T0308537

Collected Poems
Gerard Fanning

First edition

Poems © Gerard Fanning Estate, 2024
Introduction © Gerald Dawe Estate, 2024
Afterword © Colm Tóibín, 2024
Interview © Conor O'Callaghan, 2013

For permission, write to
Wake Forest University Press
Post Office Box 7333
Winston-Salem, NC 27109
wfupress.wfu.edu
wfupress@wfu.edu

ISBN 978-1-943667-15-4 (paperback)
Library of Congress Control Number 2024937426

Cover image: "Poolbeg from Clontarf" by Peter Shelley, courtesy of the photographer.
Design & typesetting by Shannon Pallatta

Publication of this book was generously supported by the Boyle Family Fund.

Collected Poems

Gerard Fanning

With an Introduction by Gerald Dawe
and an Afterword by Colm Tóibín

Edited by Conor O'Callaghan
and Bríd Ní Chuilinn

WAKE FOREST UNIVERSITY PRESS

i.m. Feargal Ó Cuilinn (1966–2017)
Béidh mé ann, béidh mé leat go deo.

Table of Contents

Introduction | Gerald Dawe   *i*

                    Easter Snow (1992)   *1*

Waiting on Lemass   *5*
August in Williamstown   *7*
Philby's Apostles on Merrion Strand   *9*
Notes on Home   .   *10*
        1. In the City   *10*
        2. The Lawn   *11*
        3. An Evening in Booterstown   *12*
        4. The Belfast Train   *13*
        5. Within a Mile of Dublin   *14*
Occupations   *15*
Alma Revisited   *17*
Making Deals   *18*
The View from Errisberg   *19*
Clifden Station   *21*
With Siobhán   *22*
Philby in Ireland   *24*
The Road to the Skelligs   *25*
Garret Barry Visits Inis Oirr   *26*
The Final Manoeuvre   *28*
Largo   *30*
Geographers   *31*
The Conquest of Djouce   *34*
Interim Memo to Getty   *36*
Mayday on Griffith Avenue   *37*
Gas   *38*
East of the Pecos   *39*
Orienteering with Elizabeth   *41*
Daytrip to Vancouver Island   *43*

Praying Mantis   45
Chemotherapy   49
Sailing into Leitrim Village, 1986   50
A Diamond for Her Throat   51
St. Charles Ward   52
Matt Kiernan   53
Unregistered Papers   54
Travelling Light   55
The Plover's Shore   56
Miller Views Los Alamos   57
Film Noir   58
Is This a Safe Place, or What?   59

Working for the Government (1999)   61

Preamble   63
July in Bettystown   67
A Cycle on Bettystown Strand   68
Laytown Races 1959   69
Alma Again   70
My Father Retires Like Terrence Malick   71
Snowstorm   72
The Fifties Parent   73
The Quaker Wall   77
Doubts Near Coosan   78
Murphy's Hexagon Revisited   79
The Bridegroom in Moycullen   80
Silence Visible on the Lough Inagh Road   81
North/West   82
About Abstraction   83
Moving into St. Vincent's Park   84
Dusk Walks   85
Shingles   86
Clare House   87
Papier-Mâché   88

Rehearsing Beckett   89

April 1963   90

Art Pepper Remembers Paul Desmond   91

St. Stephen's Day   92

Leaving Saint Helen's   94

The Erne Waters   95

Sketching Stillbirth   96

Quinsy   97

Mouth Music   98

Crop Circles   99

A Red City Journal   100

She Scratches His Wrist   103

Printing the Legend   104

Homage to George Eliot in New Hampshire   105

Working for the Government   106

Lenten Offering   107

Water & Power (2004)   109

Offering the Light   113

A Carol for Clare   114

Menzies' Field   115

Trail   117

Character in Search of an Author   118

Teepee at Bow Lake   119

The Railway Guard   120

Ludwig, Ruth & I   122

Looking Up   123

The Wards   124

First Fridays   125

I Cannot Stay   126

Stoney Road   127

The Watchers' House   128

Prayers at the Coal Quay   129

From Portstewart to Portrush   130

The Stone House: Dromod Harbour   131
Mansion House Ward   133
The Druid's Cloak   134
Like Stonehouse   135
Everything in its Place   136
The Tan Spirals   137
The Cancer Bureau   138
Searching for Paul Henry's Sky   139
Moving a Garden Shed   140
Quince   141
Water and Power   142
Wide of the Mark   143
Asylum Harbour   144
Canower Sound   147

from *Hombre: New and Selected Poems* (2011)   153

Still Man   155
A Love Story   156
An Old Boyne Fish Barn   158
Frank   159
Frost Moving   160
In My Reading   161
22/09/07   163
Head the Ball   164
Low Tide   166
Magazine   168
No Going Back   169
Toss   170
Preston's   171
Tate Water   172
Thompson & Thompson   173
That Note   174
White Page   175
The Verandah   176

The Silent Brother 177
Variation on Blue Note 179
Waking Tom 180
Weekend Away 181
What Maureen Knew 182
Who Speaks 183
Newfoundland Time 184

Slip Road (2017) 185

Mischief at the Globe 187
Ballynahinch Station 189
A Shannon Boatyard 190
Those Days 192
The Blind Commute 193
Lessons in Navajo 194
And I Let It Go 195
A Lost Ball in the Long Grass 197
Tom Kilroy's Big Country 198
Orson Welles on the Ginza Line 200
After a Short Illness 201
Albrecht Dürer: Great Piece of Turf 202
Ard Na Mara 203
Bernadette Greevy's Last Song 205
Busby Berkeley in the Holm Oaks 206
Chaos Theory 207
False Fruit 209
For the Love of Hops 210
Greene's Bookshop and P.O. 211
Her Closed Account 212
Huston on Sartre 213
In the Footsteps of Richard Long 214
Doors Closing 216
Workshy 217
Nixer 218

Ortolan in Ballynahinch   219
Our Little Life   220
Pilgarlic   221
Rita's Version   222
Slip Road   223
Snowmelt   224
Rookery   225
Tall Boys   227
Vanlife   228
Which Side Are You On?   229
The Night Telephonist   230
Though the House is Dark   232

Afterword | Colm Tóibín   233
Interview | Conor O'Callaghan, 2013   241
Notes and Acknowledgements   253

INTRODUCTION

Gerard Fanning was born in Dublin in 1952. A graduate of University College Dublin, he worked for a time in Barcelona before joining the Irish Civil Service, with whom he worked in the Department of Social Welfare for almost forty years until taking early retirement in 2012. He published three original collections during his lifetime: *Easter Snow* (1992), *Working for the Government* (1999), and *Water & Power* (2004). There was also a chapbook entitled *Canower Sound* (2003) and a selection of previously uncollected poems in *Hombre: New and Selected Poems* (2011). This *Collected Poems* gathers for the first time all that work, along with his final unpublished collection, completed shortly before his death, into one volume arranged chronologically.

Fanning's poems were also included in *The Wake Forest Series of Irish Poetry Volume III* (2013),[1] along with an interview conducted with the editor of that anthology, poet and novelist Conor O'Callaghan, (included as an appendix to this *Collected Poems*).

Fanning was awarded the inaugural Brendan Behan Award and the Rooney Prize for Irish Literature in 1993, as well as two major literature bursaries from the Arts Council of Ireland. His poems have also been adapted by the composer Ian Wilson for his *Harbouring Suite* (2008). Gerard Fanning was preparing his fourth collection when he died on October 18th, 2017, aged sixty-five.

I

In his Preface to the third volume of the *Wake Forest Series* anthology, Conor O'Callaghan remarked that Gerard Fanning 'belongs to that shadowy enclave of civil servant poets, for whom poetry exists as a silent subversion. He does not, that I know of, participate in any "scene", and instead writes gorgeous cryptic narratives that read like pint-sized spy thrillers where protagonists travel incognito or disappear altogether'.[2]

In the brief interview that accompanies each selection of the contributor's poetry, to the question about whether or not he saw his poetry as being 'a version of secrecy, of being undercover', Fanning responded:

> [My] job is outdoors, which involves visiting businesses, interviewing and field work. It's a bit like a benign *Glengarry Glen Ross,* sharing anecdotes with colleagues; when I'm back, writing up in the office. This freedom has a maverick quality, with all the foolishness that entails. Eccentricities such as poetry are easily accommodated. If there is a covert, subversive quality to the other life of poetry, you do it in your head, on the bus, observing all the time. The job stuff is a progression from [Philip Larkin's poems] 'Toads' to 'Toads Revisited' and no harm in that.[3]

Gerard Fanning's landscape is at the core of his achievement, alongside the literary and cultural allusions which play such an abundant and enriching part in his art—a little like the Philip Larkin references in the above quotation. It is also important to keep in mind what Fanning calls 'the other life of poetry'. For if there is one thing which unites everything he has produced as a poet, the sense of poetry fulfilling 'the other life' was central to what he considered to be its *raison d'être* as an art form and the only reason for writing poetry in the first place.

And maybe the best place to start is with Fanning's family origins; the hinterland that exists in so many of his poems

is not so much the south County Dublin—in which he lived
for most of his sixty-five years—but rather the northerly
part of the county associated with his father—coastal villages
such as Bettystown, Mornington, and Laytown. These
are the places he visited and stayed as a young boy and to
which he refers in many of the poems he wrote since his
early work started to appear in the 1970s in, for example,
'New Irish Writing' of the *Irish Press*, edited by David Marcus,
and later in the *Irish Times*, under the poetry editorship of
Gerard Smyth.

In the interview to which I have already referred, Fanning
identified these places very much with a particular time of
his upbringing in the 1950s:

> The impressions laid down in those years, the colour
> and smell of the sea and the sky, barley fields stretching
> back from the dunes, horse racing on the strand, are
> like something from Alain-Fournier's novel *Le Grand
> Meaulnes*. All gone now, of course. This was the time of
> Kennedy's White House and Khrushchev's Bond villain.
> And my bald father hovering, smiling, and seeming
> to say, 'everything will be all right'. If I was too young to
> understand the Cold War, it did pervade the times, even
> in sleepy Bettystown.[4]

With poem titles such as 'July in Bettystown' and 'Laytown
Races 1959', however, and other localities name-checked, it
would be a mistake to assume that Fanning's poetry follows
the traditional Irish topographical route. Far from it. Certainly
the coastal landscapes of north counties Dublin and Meath
are etched in many of his poems, with poems about swimming,
walking the countryside, revisiting his paternal family, 'there
is no going back.'[5] But the reimagining of the past takes
on an estranging, haunted aura, capturing the mysterious
quality of interrupted time, or parallel lives; how separation
from a homeplace is never quite overcome.[6]

Among many of Fanning's fine poems of remembering, 'Ard Na Mara' displays the essential filmic or visual nature of his poetic imagination. The poem is again set in that childhood background on the northern shores of the River Boyne (and mention of 'The Neptune' is likely the local Neptune Hotel). But notice what has happened to the landscape and how it has become home to so much else—TV shows, mystery plays, French fiction, Audenesque sky-pilots, and even the everyday names of popular automobiles take on their fabulous original classical meaning.

Fanning's allusions here come from a rich seam of reading, sparked by his time as an undergraduate at University College Dublin, where his lecturers included Denis Donoghue, Thomas Kilroy, and Seamus Deane. In a brief memoir written on request,[7] Fanning painted a fascinating portrait of the poet as a very young man:

> It was September 1969, and I, 17, naïve and gauche to boot, started in University College Dublin, Earlsfort Tce., as a First Arts student. My subjects were Philosophy, Political Economy and English. At the time, that area of Dublin—Earlsfort Tce., Leeson Street and St. Stephen's Green—was wonderfully irreverent and lively. There were student boarding houses, squalid bed-sits, draughty flats, Alexandra College in its posh secluded grounds, St. Vincent's Hospital and a bunch of public houses that seemed to be packed all day. And on a string of soon-to-be-demolished 19th-century tenements leading up to the University, someone had scrawled—'Desolation Row'.

> The formidable Prof. Denis Donoghue presided over the English Department. A serious man, we knew he was in constant correspondence with the movers and shakers of American Literature (now there is 'a collected letters' worth publishing) and had only a passing interest in the

local scene. At each academic year start, he perceived as his primary duty to shatter the complacency of new undergraduates, so the Michaelmas Term would consist of prosody and more prosody. But we also knew that a brilliant, young Northern lecturer, Seamus Deane, had joined the Department the previous year. Professor Donoghue's mood seemed to have lightened. At last, here was someone with whom he could really converse.

Seamus Deane was marvellous and exhilarating in the lecture theatre. We were to study Jane Austen (*Emma*) and Albert Camus (*The Plague*) amongst others. There was perfection here, and it was up to us to identify, contextualise and then hold dear for the rest of our lives. The lectures were mesmerising. He seemed to start with the bones of a thesis, but as he walked up and down by the lectern, new ideas, associations and tentative conclusions would spark and collide He effortlessly made the sociological, ethical, ontological and economic strands of his evolving argument cohere into a formidable thesis, only to deconstruct his argument, begin again, and offer counter interpretations. And all conducted as if he took us seriously, a conversation between equals.

We were to believe that he trusted us to keep up, and trusted us with the same thought processes. Being First Arts, and the winnowing not yet complete, lectures were held in the largest theatre available, but two more theatres were always on stand-by to relay the lectures with loudspeakers. There might have been some slippage in attendance at some of Desmond Connell's metaphysical ramblings in the Philosophy Dept., but not with Seamus Deane. We knew he was part of that miraculous grouping from Northern Ireland (Heaney, Mahon etc.), and his first poetry collections would appear in the 70s and 80s.

In my second year I dropped English to pursue a degree in Philosophy & Economics. The Arts Faculty moved out to Belfield, St. Vincent's Hospital moved to Elm Park, Alexandra College moved to Milltown. That once vibrant area of Dublin relaxed into its present anonymity—ghosts of junior doctors, nurses in uniform and posh school girls, forever young, flitting into bar back rooms and snugs, long gone. But Seamus Deane made that time bright for many of us, raising literature to an exploded view, seeing Shakespeare as our contemporary and positing the University as a real place for the imagination.

Fanning did not have to go far when UCD made that move to Belfield. Living in what he termed 'our middle-class upbringing in Mount Merrion',[8] he recalled how in the sixties, 'in the summer we would have swam down in the Blackrock Baths, and our Dad Barney was always bringing us to the Stella cinema to watch Westerns'. This sense of place attaches itself to both aesthetic and civil questions. Responding to a comment from Conor O'Callaghan about 'water and seeing' and 'the draw to light and water' in his work, Fanning remarked: 'it's where I live, the sea nearly always in view, the memory of foghorns, a cruel history of shipwreck and drowning and the harbour at Dún Laoghaire with its relics of empire and emigration. The changing light now seems less a feature of what we live in and more of a miracle, to be celebrated out of the everyday'.[9]

In his poem 'Asylum Harbour', for example, he captured best the traces of this history with the neighbouring townscape of Dún Laoghaire, a poem commissioned by the Harbour Commissioners and etched in stone along the Dún Laoghaire promenade overlooking Dublin Bay.

Dublin, however, is not the only point of contact for Fanning's poems. There is his increasingly intimate relationship with the west of Ireland, based around his time working in Clifden, and his subsequent visits to Connemara, rendered in the sequence 'Canower Sound'. His infatuation with French literature and fascination with Paris and Beckett's presence there surfaces in several poems, as well as his abiding knowledge of and love for American literature, film, and popular music. His reading was catholic and highly influenced by the economic and social opening up of the Republic in the 1970s.

Fanning went on to read and savour the poetry of Eavan Boland, Thomas Kinsella, Seamus Heaney, Derek Mahon, and Michael Longley, alongside his beloved Elizabeth Bishop and Philip Larkin. As already mentioned, he identified at UCD the influential role of Seamus Deane, but also diplomat and poet Richard Ryan, as well as undergraduate contemporaries who became lifelong friends, including Colm Tóibín and the late Patrick King, also a published poet, among other friends he worked with and socialized with over many years and for whom the highs and lows of the Ireland football squad were meat and drink to unending conversation.

II

It may well be true to say that the critical reception for Gerard Fanning's poetry was much more congenial outside Ireland than within, notwithstanding the acknowledgement which came with the awarding of (in particular) the Rooney Prize for Irish Literature.

Katharine Washburn, the American editor, 'looking transatlantically at this engaging work' in her review[10] of *Working for the Government* (and Vona Groarke's *Other People's*

Houses), was fascinated by Fanning's word choice, an issue that produced an unlikely exchange of letters about meanings of words in the same newspaper. 'Fanning's second collection', she wrote, 'is elegantly published by Dedalus, but some typographical errors... create a problem in the close reading required of his musical and supple line':

> Where a title poem can often be trusted to unlock the entrance to a work, or disclose some larger intention, *Working for the Government* left me reeling on the threshold. Fanning's preamble already warns us of a poet 'like a limpet recording its fastidious journeys'. A limpet is indeed a 'marine gastropod clinging to rocks with its low conical shell always open beneath'—perhaps a good listener, but not the most communicative of creatures.
>
> The title poem is on its way to a more forbidding statement, given our understanding of the work of bureaucracies as mysterious, inscrutable and indecipherable except to a few initiates with access to the codebook. In one of his best poems, 'A Red City Journal', Fanning asks: What are these signatures that cannot be undone? then remarks:
> We guard our language like a foreign tongue.
>
> So he does. There's nothing wrong with a poet's use of a technical lexicon, drawn from some special expertise, when it's consistent and discrete, but the 'pellmet', the 'femerell', the 'callows' and the 'guillemot' don't issue from the same vocabulary. I still don't know what this persuasive talent, promising so much but leaving the reader parched and befuddled, has on his mind. His limpet is hanging fast to some slippery rock, muttering an exotic word for a censer: ('thurible'), and guarding his secrets. Fanning is too gifted to scrounge for words like

'contrails' just to invoke crystals from the atmosphere. The civil service is a hermetic trade, but why should the author of the lovely 'She Scratches His Wrist' imitate its worst habits of language: the mingy and the costive? Poets have a licence to rummage the dictionaries of the recondite, if so they choose, but to mingle them so recklessly to obtain an impenetrable polyglot patois raises a further barrier to a talent which already reveals too little of its purpose.

...The fluent and accomplished Gerard Fanning paces broad fields, an enigmatic surveyor with an appetite for the exotic cultivar. ...To whom are they speaking so subtly and so well, but with a resonance subdued into near silence?

Since the review appeared in 1999, Fanning's poems were to find a home in the *London Review of Books*.[11] It is also worth noting that English critics have been much more receptive to the cadences of his poetry. In the *Guardian,* for instance, Sarah Crown heralded *Water & Power* for the manner in which Fanning:

anchors his meditative, often dreamlike poetry in the physical world with a mixture of evocative place names (Ballynahinch Lake, Cape Spear, Coal Quay) and highly specialised, often archaic language that had me reaching more than once for the dictionary. Roof beams are 'purlins'; in the course of reading the collection I discovered that 'salal' is a low-growing shrub and 'ogham' an ancient alphabet consisting of parallel strokes. These alluringly abstruse words contribute to the strangeness of poems in which the metaphors as well as the vocabulary are frequently ambiguous; the pleasingly enigmatic picture of 'The tickertape of frightened stock / That utters from the weathervane', for example, is visually vivid but unexplicated, leaving room for the reader's own thoughts. By and large, these are melancholy poems, run through with threads of memory, anxiety, illness and loss. But despite their sobriety, they contain moments of real glory. In 'The Stone House: Dromod Harbour', one of the finest poems in the collection, Fanning succeeds in endowing death with an almost ethereal grace when he transforms a suicide into 'a man who was falling, / ... Folding his wings'. In images such as this, the quiet power of his unassuming style is exemplified.[12]

While the English poet and scholar Fiona Sampson considered how the same collection:

ends by reclaiming the beauty of the physical world. 'Canower Sound', the sequence which makes up the second part of this book, shows us the poet's mastery of the surprising in both language and image—'the shag and slime of stones', 'a wind plays "long fetch" to the waterline'—but it's a mastery which, as the poet's familiar advises him, 'strike out in a languid freestyle'. That ghost, Stonehouse the escape artist, urges both poet—and, by extension, reader—to 'Make it up as you go along'; and Fanning's loose-limbed verse, with its understated rhyme and comfortable diction, might at first glance seem to do just that. But these quietly spoken poems are constructions of extreme delicacy, alert to the shifts of air and spirit. It is this delicacy which allows them to range an expansive geography while continuing their exploration of inwardness.

For, as poems such as 'The Cancer Bureau' and 'Wide of the Mark' make explicit, the deeper music of the book sounds a brush with mortality. In perhaps the most shocking and tender of these pieces, 'The Wards', Fanning evokes the fragility of the protection offered by intensive care: 'After the final blizzard I found her head / lying among the strings of the tent'. This register of courage and clarity helps return us to the opening poem of a remarkably cyclic book, in which the poet's final glance round a twilit cricket ground, after a metaphorical 'poor light stopped play', is 'one more entry' in a retrospect of life itself.[13]

Selecting Fanning's *Working for the Government* as one of his Books of the Year for 1999, novelist Colm Tóibín, Fanning's UCD contemporary and friend, noted how '[t]hese poems combine a tone that is intimate and urgent with a formal reticence and an absolute care and respect for language.'[14] Further afield, Fanning gave a reading from *Hombre* at the 2013 International Association for the Study of Irish Literatures Japan (IASIL Japan), hosted by Kyoto Notre Dame University. The event and the collection were later reviewed by Peter Cheyne:

> I will give my impressions in support of my heartily recommending this volume [*Hombre*] to all poetry lovers… The poems are meditative, sometimes playful, and they successfully transport the reader to a thoughtful, general, and calm place. 'General' is an unusual word to be used in praise of poetry, but…Fanning's meditative art attends to and plays with genera in a haunting and most intriguing way. …Yet Fanning's awareness of dangerous undercurrents is balanced, in these intimate poems, with kind-hearted wit and gently suggestive word play.[15]

Cheyne continues to recount how, 'in his talk… Fanning said that he named the volume after one of his favourite Western movies, *Hombre* (1967), directed by Martin Ritt and starring a very laconic Paul Newman':

Fanning's favouring this Western film, with its stylishly sparse dialogue and its emphasis on conveying meaning through direct symbolism and action, perhaps tells of his fascination with Ludwig Wittgenstein. In his student days at University College Dublin, in the 1960s and early 1970s, Fanning absorbedly read Wittgenstein. Nevertheless the connections that most made sense to him were the existential traits in the novels of such authors as Dostoevsky, Gide, and Camus. 'Undergraduate, adolescent angst perhaps', Fanning relates in conversation, 'but fertile nonetheless.' For the early-period Wittgenstein, all the really important things—God, the soul, ethics, and aesthetics—are best expressed wordlessly if one is careful to avoid corrupting ineffable value into nonsense. The early Wittgenstein's conviction is consonant with the spartan, resolute *Hombre* and, I think, with Fanning's meditative poetry.

The reviewer goes on to make a fascinating link between Wittgenstein and Fanning's poetry:

The philosopher concluded his *Tractatus-Logico Philosophicus* asserting, 'Whereof one cannot speak, thereof one must be silent'... Nonetheless, the poet may sing without explaining, and may imaginatively show without having to tell, and Fanning accomplishes both with a characteristic sense of fun... Fanning's play is meaningful, but it is play, and he advances no theses... A gentleness of spirit, then, and a love of meaningful form and the evocative pulses of thought and feeling are embodied throughout the poems in this collection. It is this playful, gentle quality, balanced with the obscure, evocative, and powerfully fluid undercurrents of thought and mood that make *Hombre* a highly recommended and exciting volume of poetry.

In an interview with Seán Rocks for RTÉ's *Arena* to mark the publication of *Hombre* in 2011, Fanning spoke of the importance of music in his poetry.[16] From Matt Kiernan, the traditional Uilleann piper, to Lucia Popp, the Slovakian soprano, Dexter Gordon, the great American jazz tenor saxophonist, Fanning's poetry is simply alive to the majesty of song and sounds. This sound-system echoes with numerous writerly presences, and the cinematic world finds in Fanning's poems a backlist the likes of which few other contemporaries can match: Louis Malle, John Ford, Federico Fellini, and John Huston. Filmmakers and films provide Fanning with a creative background within which the emotional and visual world he inhabits is revealed with deft, imaginative touches. The key to the achievement of his poetry resides in Fanning's strong and long-lasting attachment to places, his heartlands.

These are Irish, most certainly, but they also include Paris, to which he was drawn, and the culture of North America in which he was deeply informed of its literature, music, and, of course, cinema. Fanning played no part in the old-fashioned Irish literary parlour game of pitting Ireland against Europe, the local against the sophisticated other. He saw this self-mythologizing through the prism of a highly intelligent yet sensual attention to the human condition and a philosophical subtlety which is perhaps becoming increasingly more uncommon today. That said, there was not a nostalgic note in his imaginative frame of reference.

He was very much a man of his time and saw the cultural and religious changes within his own place as necessary and liberating while being very conscious of the economic and moral issues residing within the Irish Catholic class system, a topic I have heard him speak on with real anger in his voice. But Fanning's poetry is cloudless with little political overcast.

Despite the health issues he faced from his teenage years, there is no hint of self-pity. The stoical temperament, in fact, was neatly offset by a self-ironizing attitude, some of which I have touched upon here. Fanning the poet focused every-thing upon, to use a concept from the Anglo-Irish novelist and philosopher Iris Murdoch, 'the unselfing' of the individual condition or plight. 'The self, the place where we live, is a place of illusion', Murdoch wrote. 'Goodness is connected with the unself, to see and to respond to the real world in the light of a virtuous consciousness'.[17]

Fanning's elaborate and detailed notebooks and journals (now housed in the John J Burns Library, Boston College) reveal a poet of exceptional reflection and thoughtfulness who worked hard at what he saw as the key to poetic value; attention to the lived world had to be, in his practice, matched by formal control; form, in other words. Language use was what mattered most, the music and timbre of voice and tone, even to the sardonic point of self-parody. For who else could find a word such as 'Pilgarlic' and make such a poem using it?

In a rare foray into reviewing—Fanning found writing prose an ordeal—he produced a fascinating little 'notice' of the poet he most admired above all others and took great enjoyment and inspiration from—Paul Muldoon. In celebrating Muldoon's collection *Horse Latitudes* (2006), Fanning inadvertently identifies the very elements which a keen and ready reader can see and hear in his own verse:

> Paul Muldoon is a force of nature. His 10th collection, *Horse Latitudes,* may show signs of middle age spread, but his music, tone and delight in language remain razor sharp. That his sleep-fuelled thoughts, on waking, could turn him into a poetry machine, might signal danger, or whatever makes him riff obsessively through 'something

else, then something else again' lead to flippancy, has been well documented. But it's worth the ride. Twenty years living in the US, he still pulls at the stitches of Ireland's moth-eaten fabric, writes moving elegies, inserts himself in an egg to peck out a family secret and tosses out random texts to Tom Moore. From his Princeton redoubt, from his inner room filled with dictionaries, from his love of all things contrary and the nag and pull of The Old Country—at whatever remove, we are lucky to have him. This is a marvellous book.[18]

In conclusion, I would turn the tables and say that, 'from his love of all things' and 'the nag and pull of The Old Country', we are indeed lucky to have had a poet of Gerard Fanning's grace and insight and attentiveness, as this *Collected Poems* abundantly reveals. Above all else, we can marvel at his marvellous poems which await the student and general reader who has the time and curiosity to enter Fanning Country. They will not be disappointed.

– *Gerald Dawe*

Notes

1. Conor O'Callaghan, ed. *The Wake Forest Series of Irish Poetry Volume III* (Winston-Salem, NC: Wake Forest University Press, 2013).
2. *The Wake Forest Series*, xvii.
3. *The Wake Forest Series*, 187.
4. *The Wake Forest Series*, 188.
5. See Fanning's poem 'No Going Back' on page 169.
6. See 'The Railway Guard', 120.
7. Quoted in Gerald Dawe, 'History Lessons: Derek Mahon & Seamus Deane', in *The Wrong Country: Essays on Modern Irish Writing* (Newbridge: Irish Academic Press, 2018), 89–91
8. 'Gerard and Dave Fanning: Siblings', *Irish Times*, 23 October 2004.
9. *The Wake Forest Series*, 195.
10. Katharine Washburn, 'To Whom are they speaking so subtly and so well, but with a resonance subdued into near silence?' *Irish Times*, 19 June 1999.
11. Gerard Fanning, 'Rookery', 4 January 2018; 'The Blind Commute', 28 July 2016; Two

Poems, 2 August 2007; and 'The Stone House: Dromod Harbour', 16 November 2000.

12. Sarah Crown, 'Examinations of birds and words', *Guardian*, 21 January 2006.

13. Fiona Sampson, 'A brush with mortality', *Irish Times*, Weekend, 19 February 2005, 10.

14. Colm Tóibín, 'Who Read What', *Irish Times*, 4 December 1999.

15. Peter Cheyne, review of *Hombre: New and Selected Poems*, by Gerard Fanning, *Journal of Irish Studies* 29 (2014): 67–69.

16. Seán Rocks interviews Gerard Fanning: https://www.rte.ie/radio1/arena/programmes/2017/1019/913755-arena-thursday-19-october-2017/?clipid=102636083

17. Iris Murdoch, 'The Sovereignty of Good over Other Concepts', in *Existentialists and Mystics: Writings on Philosophy and Literature,* ed. Peter Conradi (London: Penguin Books, 1997), 376.

18. Gerard Fanning, 'A selection of paperbacks reviewed', *Irish Times*, 3 November 2007.

Easter Snow

1. The Conquest of Djouce

WAITING ON LEMASS

It is nineteen sixty-two
or -three, and we are playing soccer
in fields laced with the sheen of bamboo.

In the air that turns
amber like sally rods,
somewhere out of picture

a man is hitting golf balls
as if there was no tomorrow.
He slouches towards the sycamore shade

searching for what couples
might be lying in the seed beds
or that tall grass

loosely flecked with rye.
None the wiser, we walk home
under the beige satellites

that roll in the ether of themselves,
while all about,
a blaze of radio perfume

speaks of a man
moving his ships on soup-like waters,
or a president slumped

on his girlfriend's knee,
as here our long druid leaders
wander through the closing zones,

their autistic god
commanding options in the street,
the curfew till the white hour.

AUGUST IN WILLIAMSTOWN

I watch the white moon rising,
a tantalising spark of God's benign face
revelling in our bewildered eyes.

As I walk, owls croon,
and a wide grin of scent cruises
in the lawn's lavish spaces.

Moving down through Wicklow's
stretching estates, slipping into
the mask of ease, I grasp

a tended landscape, bordered gardens —
elements I can understand.
Even Calary, desolate and ice-clear

in the dwindling autumn light
welcomes me. I am at home.
See this smile —

it perfects my dual life,
a sinner erasing sin
I spend six months in the odour

of prayer, while my face shrinks
from this chalice. If, occasionally
I head for the city, I slide

like the moon through thin branches
down the too crowded streets.
There I recall cold flagstones

a perpetual murmuring, and stare
at living gods, their smiles
resigned to a surfeit.

PHILBY'S APOSTLES ON MERRION STRAND

All of these beaches—
mist drenched in wide lagoons—
were drawn out neatly for cartographers.

Why then do men come
hauling seismometers, their tripods
straining for the lateral view?

Silently they position
to observe the wing-beat migrations
of a city's carriages.

They may as well define
the waves gasping breath
as they check for new terminals,

for here they have come
to the outer limits,
tracing the flaw in the rounded eye,

the fault in the world's Chippendale.
Watch them tune their cackling radios
of bird-song and wind-song,

staring eastward as though
a life's objective could ring less clear
down the crowded airwaves.

Meanwhile a world of talking heads
passes their door; quiet manoeuvres
belie hidden purpose.

NOTES ON HOME

1. In the City

The city stays awake all night
sparked in occasional carlight
and we lie down, together or alone
as all the metals groan
or purr to a dead stop.

In single rooms, phones idling,
we dream out across
rooftops, empty warehouses
where lost consignments
still flash aimlessly
on a raised map of the world.

Through the workings
of a city's widening parishes
cruising taxis waltz,
eyes diminishing in a dawn rise
of radios and banging screens.

And we rise
waking in the bright shuffle
of paperthin messages
brought down the icy roads
to these, our halls
and silent window boxes.

2. The Lawn

Hoe the black clay till its spur
resembles the dust of the moon map,
let all the sandy seas mirror the pantry floor
and let the calm that follows down
play through the agonies
of the fickle pollen storms.
Might everything find its level –
field-cow wheat, dandelion and thistle,
the grain and the tassel of a sage trampoline?
Now as shooting stars descend
I correct small contour flaws,
pencil-stroke a declining magic
on the staves for the next rendition,
and dream of a pine needle perfection
where your hint might be the blueish vein,
the charcoal in the bush soul,
the resin nibbling the membrane.

3. An Evening in Booterstown

After cold days taking photographs
confirming the nearest coastline,
I look from your window
and see how the tramp fields
have turned to a wax impression
of the sea's other shores. Reclining
like a folded mirror, or growing
in detail just as these blank papers
on the tray near the alcove
swim in their blue chemicals,
they gather the last of Dublin's
refracted light. See there
emerging from the covering darkness
of lintels, bay-windows and shut
doors, another circle of light corrects
the skyline. Like any brief town
time has polished it, with
the sea-marsh and the harbour wall,
to a pale permanence.

4. The Belfast Train

Though we don't set our watches anymore
we note the temporary withdrawals
and file the small faults
in a flawless system. Round Dundalk

tracks may remain empty for days—
the ghostly carriages wintering
in the blank fields. Word gets through,
buses awkwardly skirt the pocket miles.

If we sit till we comprehend
like gangers repairing the timetables,
we may think the random suicides
are powdered with pockmarks

and tossed beneath the train
as an afterthought. Or, if lives
in the stilt-house junction boxes
tick out their last

in a whispering discontent,
the automatic levers are watched
yet working on
whistling through the late departures.

5. Within a Mile of Dublin

Waiting for the new ice age
a fifties rucksack slung in the hall,
panniers fading into survival,
and here a bureau filled with maps –
all the bright cities that spiral out
from the paving stones of parishes
to the glass of the world savannah.

See how my child-like drawings
foretold the smoky photographs
that swam through faded oxygen,
and see how I pretend to know
the swirl of the earth's weather,
the politics of dwindling satellites –
trying to imagine the lost caresses
meandering in space. So if I draw
boundaries ravenous for acreage
I still remember where the coffee-
stained villages are breathing
beneath the listless reservoirs.

OCCUPATIONS
Germans over Belfast, 1941

From the high sun of Germany
we climb into the dark,
a steel pack of light diviners.

Below, our giant homeland
cautiously gathers the seas,
trains the sun and smiles up

at our glinting journeys. Perhaps
her wise stare will chart
the blank no-man's land

which rides down on us
from the cold north; for clearly
the world is a closing fist.

Europe's hinge tightening
as we veer north from Dublin.

Outside, the constant radar unfurls
like a red spool of brain –
picks out pocketed holdings,

mild couplings and lights
crawling up the narrow roads.

This sleepy tackle of stars
is their Maginot Line,
a honeycomb of drowned valleys

eating through the land
like a changeling crop
yielding to its own seasons.

In the confused fires we build
a tatter of signals:
our life's definition now,

a tired odyssey in a world
grown warm with our cold grip.

ALMA REVISITED

No trace of the north marsh polder,
the hooker sloops off Rush,
the girl reading under the verandah.

I could lay Saint-Exupéry aside,
and search like his swab biplane
for that polyester strip.

But I wake, and the loop round the bawn
shows the hotel not yet extended.
In *Ard Na Mara, Lisheen Villa,*

a mild bel canto voice
fills the tented air with soothing sleep,
while you stand on Ford-strewn beaches,

in a bitter quail light,
characters from a dust bowl depression,
smiling despite the terror of the future.

MAKING DEALS

Landscape painters, photographers,
have us standing awkwardly
ignoring the image maker—
it's only half a lie,

for we are the ciphers
that give you what you see.

All round the growing cold streets
men are making deals.
They meet in bars, hush,
bend heads and gesture

in the underhand.
Within their splayed fingers
the cluttered microfilm exchange
of blueprints passed

all in the ease
of casual conversation.

Where we made the streets
gaps became alleyways
and men rode out in cars
to marshal the intelligence

of addresses. Now as money
abandons the derelict sites
they circle on stilts
attempting to cohere the subterfuge.

Watch as the centre slowly hollows
and cables map the countryside.

THE VIEW FROM ERRISBEG

Robert Lloyd Praeger
called it the best in Ireland.
Climbing with three children

where ice or bulldozed shale
must have wrestled with form,
I saw the thunder of the North West Passage

pouring into a pagan bowl,
and through a muslin sheen of horseflies
I gazed like Praeger

at the magnificent loneliness of the lakes.
Weeks later in a cowering Dublin,
I stand in a blue light

and watch the smoky figure
begin to emerge,
my long lost Franklin,

whose loneliness charged the incidental
into a world-weary search
for a safe passage

out of God's bleak stare.
I stack the inky photographs —
engraved miniature journeys —

and sense wild indigo
peppering my skin,
prompting a medical note

or a bruised tattoo
to rise from the cracked calamine
for all the lost galleons

moaning on their beds of brine.
Perhaps a leisured life
becomes its own fabric,

as here in braided light,
place-names fade with the ochre sun,
my folded map tucks like an alpenstock

and I drift into the lull of mid-evening,
dreaming of an astronaut
who descends through hoar frost,

his visor blank with detail,
all the thin bleached drawings
of our winter trading ships

locked in the purple ice;
and already in the *National Geographic*
the mock-up is conceived.

CLIFDEN STATION

I ride the necklace of roads
on this island
but never reach the·sea.
All around me hollow stretches
topple into the evening sun
and the sky begins
to fall again with frost.

I try, as I can, to understand
these wintry acres —
a soldier's nightmare of no cover,
looted trucks cradling the ditches as
mild corrosions burn the moon-white fields.

Above me, the whining transit planes
circle like the night's static —
a million voices on my radio.
I skirt the perimeters of stations,
the yellow main streets,
searching for some treeless rendezvous
where messages transfer.

WITH SIOBHÁN

We walk sluicing these rainfields
talking of other people
never ourselves, as if
growing side by side in the actual
were all that was.

Yet see there
like a lunar diagram
or there
like a breast behind calico –
the lines of other lives.

In these bald fields
chambered graves
reveal like an x-ray's grey definition
God's face staring back –
a shadow on the Andes slopes.

Here is a litter trove of ingenuity
layered like floor panelling
beneath the ground.
Overnight abandoned mines
clink and gleam

endless highways
buckling in a rich seam.
And where I have left you
walking on alone
I see the waggon trails

where they hauled
the teepee stones,
a village of homage
to a god
as bright as our own.

PHILBY IN IRELAND

Nightfall, and we have driven out
from the warm lights. The thick fog
circling the hill's base corrodes
our white car as it stalks the incline.

From this high air we can see
the crawling streets, trucks and buses
wheeling in their correct motions—
trails leaving a decipher of rests.

Somewhere in this parallel of workings
men catalogue the labyrinth of the city,
and deep in its crushed underbelly
we meet and copy the blueprints

of a world drawn out on long papers.
Lives collapse if we fail, for our work,
though underhand, is significant.
Like priests we are diligent or we do not

believe. Abandoning cars, we move down
to the murmuring inlets, wide lagoons
cheeping at the breaker wall. We sail out
adrift in the wider perspective.

THE ROAD TO THE SKELLIGS

We have outstayed our welcome.
Taking only what we can carry
we walk south, a geiger sense
of food and survival building

in our prayers a brief taste
of God's companionship. He sends all.
Yet daily see how our sacrifices refine
to the practical. These planned escapes

are far removed from the passive
Latin incantations that struggle
in a previous intelligence.
As if to deny us now the ocean

rises, while the rain's waltzing feet
tripples islands in the image
of our amazed stores of gold
melting to a powder of foam.

Slowly the road is giving in.
Even here it steeplejacks to the rim
of a saucer bog and falls
down into the Glen's mouth

where the Skelligs flicker—
a monstrance jagged with rare stone.
We will sail the drowned valley
in prayer, safe from God and man.

GARRET BARRY VISITS INIS OIRR

My eyes sink to the ticking clock
of a thumping currach
straddling the sea; muffled conversations

surround me in this cloudy bowl.
Sitting on a low stool
in the sunlit doorway,

crayon light halves the room,
turf smoke, pipe smoke,
cradling the drawn faces

appearing before me. As I play
my eyes shut like a silent hall
cool and envious of the sun,

while my father's music
builds in harmonies
colliding in my memory.

I hone timbres of foot tappings,
the fussy sounds of dancers' feet
like a tuning orchestra,

release the stopped air
of this compact church organ
resting on my knee. Glossed round

the old men at the hedgerows
I see the map of future tunes,
and further through the shawled fields—

the incomprehensible beauties
of the lake roads; mountain silence
a perfect sound, I perfect it.

THE FINAL MANOEUVRE

Living the middle life,
caught between lovers,
I was prepared for the holocaust

that never came.
Crossing years like days
on a schoolboy's calendar,

tracking without retreat,
I was the inexorable traveller
pursuing my wounded grail.

On that chill November evening
in Glenmalure, I could have owned
the whole of Wicklow

but fences would have encouraged thieves.
So, turning in this cocoon
of soft noises

I stare smiling
toward the spark of the living,
their coloured flags weaving

a cosy fever, their loves
chased by clock hands
and a life's debris.

Lying in this damp chair,
a festering in the moor-swamp's side,
I draw a pulled curtain of hair

to keep the seasons in ebb-tide,
while this axle of earth
conceals me, composes my relief.

LARGO

They found a body in the uplands,
a village sleeper, curled in the furred snow,
not caring to go on.

When we examine the ice-clean repose
a chill seeps through the jerkin sleeve,
the wire glasses telescope a score of winters,

and the padding of a strip of pine
becomes the blip in the earlobe
attaching to his heart's pace.

Might we also carry our saline bag
over the loughs and tarot,
a journey through the fleecy undertow,

past the crossroads post office,
where pension money and stamps
watermark to a like regret?

Or perhaps, if we peered into the hard lime
that freezes the channels in the trees,
we too could stare back admiring it all—

the world events comically coming apart,
and love, the measure of our lives,
billeted one month for every year.

GEOGRAPHERS

1.

Dragonflies dart
in the earth's smoke
as we race up country.
The road is a crucifix

of turns, wind
a dull chant
pulling us to the Boyne
and beyond.

When we reach
the white-washed
courtyards of Meath,
its silent tumuli are

drifting and the mist
sprawls a white coverlet
screening their bright dance.
In dense, loud bars

we sense the waves'
pocketed beatings,
and careering in
the moon's soft tug

we toss the harsh music.
Outside, in the cold glow
of the world, frost
crafts glass and cobbles

to topography, and further
through a running contour
of mounds and clay crosses
a cluster of larks

sing dreary lullabies
to their unborn. It reaches us
as faint voices
maddening comprehension.

2.

Perhaps the drizzle
will subside
and we will map
that village of grass;

meantime like monks
we make jealous copy
of their neat
choir's discipline,

build an inventory
of the composer's silence—
for as quiet musicians
our wasted lives are spent

farming a stolen pasture,
giving orders
in a lost tongue.
In our haste

we have left this village
behind and the path
through the fields
locks to a gold brooch

of indecision,
pinning to the ground's
bruised skin its curled
loam. We must begin

again, trust only
the earth's booming,
straining to detail
its mechanism.

If, suckling on the mind's
music, we grow a tougher mime,
then we can sharpen
the tongue's reed,

imagine a space—
the wild dens
we dream about,
contented silence.

THE CONQUEST OF DJOUCE

Even on the simplest journey
doubts may cloud the familiar.
Consider the walk from Djouce

down to the barnyard of the world;
hauling sextants, compasses
and a dull stevedore calm,

we can't conceive of lost cargoes,
or how pot-bellied planes
could fail and slowly condense

in a swelter of rambling vine.
Yet miles from radio signals,
the morse that brings up the day,

land dreams of the human gaze.
For there is only a view, a scattering of tan,
broken fences rusting into local colour

and for twenty miles around,
pluming fires in the cinnamon sky.
Where Powerscourt mulls in distant heat,

Burton or Speke might rise to stare
from their floating canopy of malaria.
They could imagine the Nile

meandering down the page to its legend.
But Djouce is just what it seems—
a downy floor transmitting to elsewhere

the arc of our particular North Star,
and the boundaries are occasional,
like the fleece that translates appearances

into the cumulus of the view.
The evening coming slowly in
trails our bivouac through the ozone,

and the figure waving like a metronome
is *the Eskimo in his skin canoe,*
the only one who ever came through.

INTERIM MEMO TO GETTY

I should write about the long walk
down from Mount Brown,

the pension visit, living alone enquiries,
dust streets and tenements,

the handhold and foothold
where Magritte might confuse

a windowsill with a chimney breast,
or watch the floral wallpaper surround

xeroxed across the sky.
But I sit all day in your open-plan,

watching men point from a building site,
fill their geometry in tinsmith columns

so the rising scaffold of corridors
can store the heat of the sun.

Perhaps the frost that gathers round us all
confuses the act with its document,

as the sliding past, the fabulous seepage,
drains from private meter rooms

and our world sways in the air
on arms of glass intrigue.

MAYDAY ON GRIFFITH AVENUE

The Irish Sea sweats like a benign lake
in this midnight heat, two miles off.
Where asphalt merges with steel
and car-fins part the rain trees,
I dream of the ocean's rising,
how small effects like some insect genocide
has the sea mildly pouring here,
over lawns, railed basements;
and while the edgy foam and spirit level
shunts in the city's sidings,
all the scattered families watch
the swaying sun in their elsewhere,
the threat in the wounded stratosphere.

GAS

A man is taking readings
of pump and pressure
as the red fanlight,
that bloom in the western sky,
comes down from all around.

The last cars map the globe
as he checks the oilcans,
the switch on *Mobilgas,*
and settles in the lee alcove
where his soft-back thriller
waits in its glove of chrome.

If he bothers to lock the outhouse
he will see how someone has scrawled
a message on the washroom mirror.

EAST OF THE PECOS

I live in the city manager's
inherited dream,
far from the badlands
sagebrush and sombrero

of the sierra foothills,
rather the cap and lavender face
towelled to a neat complexion.
Out from the plywood shavings

all the new line houses
spreadeagle and recline,
a treeless prairie
in its first winter:

children stopping screaming
joggers setting out
or coming into land
and overhead the teatime flight

from Heathrow, bored executives
looking down on us.
Each night, road lights
trigger with the dark

family cars homing exhausted
to their thin white shrouds,
while Howth Head scrambles
the excited signals

from the North,
and lapsing in our private dreams
we covet the blue imaginings,
the spark and metal

out over the Irish Sea.
As world events
break more violently,
I check the bus journeys,

the train's halt,
the road that slowly fills with cars
and marvel at natural manoeuvres undisturbed.
Each morning we wait

and all the minor details
of our future are retold
as though the world could possibly know
its own course

depending on us merely
to ride out in the choreography
of lightning touches,
while contracting streets

blunder like moths to the greens,
a trail boss eye, fixed
for the railway, the jug of commerce
and the saddle-weary horizon.

ORIENTEERING WITH ELIZABETH

Here is the report of a man
walking out to the white valleys,
breathing the mind-expanding air

of that blind corrie
which might hide the North Pole,
and carrying nothing

but the webbed gauze of himself.
I would give him
a radio filled with static,

a glowing stencil of food stations
and some whispered ingenuity
to fend the air of the laconic tundra.

But why leave the land of the living
when echoes of shouts
career in the deadened lines of snow,

and ice in that sheer aquamarine
swims down to the hot seas?
I am thinking now of how

you came to me one Christmas—
I showed you words
about love in the tropics

and you tensed as I reached
for the quiet sun of your breast,
wandering in the visionlines

I weakened to impress.
In the almost certainty of future,
through half sightings

you secrete the microfilm of all love
as though you knew all about
the mythical North Pole

and how it should stand
like a painting of itself
drifting in a circle of elms.

DAYTRIP TO VANCOUVER ISLAND

1.

We drove through the spine of the island,
occasional clay crosses where pockets of lives
wait for rain and the mailman.

Reclining on the invisible grain of the world,
their lock-up doors, endless gardens,
dandle like uncharted nerve ends

and screen the uncut land which must lie
where the roads are still being planned.
In a filling station, burning *Mobilgas*

I bought a card of Mount St. Helens
hoping to send it to you,
a slight tremor to conceal

like the shy scooped up lunar dust
or the ash that basks hereabout
in a relaxed stare, on temperance houses,

Salvation Army platforms
and the batten wooden concaves
of the various sun worshippers.

2.

The sea at Victoria was no surprise—
couples promenading, gazing at Japan,
horizons defined in snug harbour lights

all mapped, all comprehended
like the fading zones of space.
Nightfall, and we rode the ferry

back to our miniature selves
caught smiling on the mantelpiece,
delighted it could be so simple.

Elizabeth, Elizabeth, what can I tell you—
how the comforting life of car explorations,
or the Polaroid guide to the narrative,

ignores the constant filling of the water barrels
and the nocturnal gauze of happenings
as natural events for sleeping through?

PRAYING MANTIS

The praying mantis
is resigned to death.

Bleak stones in his eyes
are locked staring
from his brine-yellow skin.

A watching in-
sect drowsing on
the scrambler floor,

his hands are bent
in homage, body geometry
tensed and subdued.

Like a pilgrim
his lovemaking
crowds death

into a religion
with the calm and the isolate
as his safety.

He breeds on the blind
and the illogic of rarity.
Killer within the law.

I am an outlaw
if I kill him.

2. Unregistered Papers

CHEMOTHERAPY

Tensing on the trip-switch of mustard gas
a pillow smell can now set off distress.
The nurse rounding my corridor of glass
holds her neat tray, her lipped capsule's largesse.

SAILING INTO LEITRIM VILLAGE, 1986

William Glenn guides us to Leitrim Village
through the cuttings that furrow off the map
along the drains and bleak pumping stations
where high water often floods
and a towpath battens down
its parodic table of love seats.
In this calm wet New Barbary,
in the days that submerge the year,
we join the chatter of leavings, great events,
where in an olive-stained drinking bar,
through the dark of Ireland's holy hour,
we drift into the words of marriage.

From this end slip
we could circle in our own length,
steer the blue margin of the marine file,
nuzzling red and black
on British government charts of another century.
But the echo-sounder bleats,
the bell-stove smokes alarmingly,
and, though the balm from the doldrums' stray fog
unfurls in the rivers and lakes,
we search for the perfect hide.
These years, letting the spirit subside,
have made us nonchalant with time.

A DIAMOND FOR HER THROAT

Your words today admonish, instruct, and coil down the page
like the seamless undulations I once showed you
of an exhausted marsh near the sea.

Might the tide here, so long gone, wait somewhere out of view,
to raise our marriage bed and trail us through
that diminishing air, that congruence of unlikely events?

I rake the mulching leaves, assorted browns of bark and carrion,
and, while October fog descends, this quiet mild surround
anticipates frost, a wrinkling quilt waiting to be tossed.

ST. CHARLES WARD

The nightwalkers drag contagion
down the long corridors.
Staring at Dublin's mailboat
they imagine the flags of the Titanic,
or its ghostly flotilla,
gliding out to formulise
the wreck of the Greenwich meridian.
However confident the world works,
days blur here,
twilight fuses the bleached phosphorescence,
taps mimic the unnamed waterfalls,
and in the corner of the room,
near the curtained sluice alcove
something bright evolves,
our menu reader slurs his lines,
my old friend is helped down
to the transplant ward,
and one by one we sign off
with a nod and a smile.

MATT KIERNAN

He tries to explain how a gift emerges
singing from the shadows, how holding
the reamer like a baton
conducts receding melodies,
and how rhythm runs
like a finger through a stencil in his brain.
The radio light trembles,
the battery bleeds in its cage,
and when at last he plays
the air is as true as the quiet inflection
of Easter snow settling in its drifts of blue.

UNREGISTERED PAPERS

With mild interrogations I prompt
computer tickings to retrieve marginalia —
obscure replies for my buff file

from the dust offices in Newcastle and Chelsea.
As though verifying the past all day
would carbon-date love's minutiae

and all this could set geigers
to predict the fahrenheit failures,
explain the meandering of the swaying sun,

or trace the moon tug that lapses
yet is endless and ascendant somewhere.
While the mosaic of tax lines assemble

my visitants flex copper-thin wrists,
and their arms splay, like the chalky sinews
of London's navvy underground.

TRAVELLING LIGHT

Before Christmas, the small gatherings
in banks and corporate offices, after hours,
mime the end-of-year parties.
I watch a brave middle-income troupe
in St. Martin-in-the-Fields
rehearse the *St. Matthew Passion,*

unseasonal scores, a birth not a death,
and momentarily forgotten,
their cars, their frail insignia,
speed underground back
to the flotilla of wharfs and gardens,
where threadbare estate lines

haphazardly define that otherness
from me and these drowsy London Irish tramps
who stretch and snore in the heated pews.
When, head in hand, your face emerges,
a young woman invoking the Messiah —
blond neck bare, strings of beads

rolled between the lynx light hairs —
I relax to imbibe that phrasing
performed time and time over,
like instinct or a commandment,
and know these sometime lines are the ties
that will reluctantly, if eventually, define.

THE PLOVER'S SHORE

Built in the Eisenhower years
when the census mercury slowed to a tilt,
our New England home

settled on its grains of bevelled glass.
Relaxing in what passes for autumn here
we stray now, like hoboes on the edge of the Atlantic

trying to find that cattleprod inlet
where some Marian monks
drill their cross with a tractor pitch

and imagine the whole wide horizon
evoked in their spirals of praying.
In the search for a dervish calm

I saw white lint rise in the air
and the silence echoed in steely beds
was the drone as names reveal the fields,

a hum detailed in the fontanelles.
Our dreams lapse in a watery doze,
they hibernate on the lake floor,

and we might be the only pair left to tell
of that ache in its silent repose,
the language of the plover's shore.

MILLER VIEWS LOS ALAMOS

The way our parishes deplete
has allowed the saplings
to multiply in the dew.

These serene colonisations
are logical strips of elm
extending to my door,

and if there is no evil intention
might some nerve
shudder in the scent of power?

Or do we all try to arrange our lives
watching one another
with mild surprise?

And if the sea should fall,
could we reinvent the horizon
or die after all?

In the swarm of tonight's radio
an awkward motif
is *Midnight in Moscow,*

yet ribbons of land
now fulfil the imagination
of Franklin's last stand.

And the parallax line
that falters in occasional fog
was there all the time.

Coyotes have appeared in the wood.

FILM NOIR

From the window of this hotel room
I see the uptown office
sweltering as it turns away from light.

Deep in the margins of these afterhours,
in the dun conveyance of apartment houses,
words like *alimony* or *realty*

animate the couple
who have just walked in from the street.
The fan has been dismantled for repair,

and, though there is latent mischief,
this is not serious.
The man who gestures to a fault

will explain the value of nothing,
and, in the time it takes to inch the door ajar,
someone teases out the frame.

IS THIS A SAFE PLACE, OR WHAT?

Even the greatness of Beechey's journeys
dims illegibly by the light in this cabin.
In the drowsy odour of kerosene
fuse elements expose,
and in the dewy interludes
where we built our seamless lives,
tears dissolve the day.
As the boat slaps on its beaded moorings,
cars thread the inlet slips
and two by two, frail magenta lights
echo music down the bones of old darkness,
setting off minute timbre bells,
that let us doze in the slippage of dreams.

We are shelved in the lea of the lough's great loves,
tied to the wooden levee—
and the hurricane lamp sauntering on the imaginary bank
could be Wolfe or Beechey
pencilling the boils on Adelaide Rock.
But is this a safe place, or what?
Do our grieving mistresses still entreat *The Times,*
pretending one more lost soul
is important in their lives?
Or are we always monitored somewhere,
just failing to return from the lakes
for the start of another week?

Working for
the Government

PREAMBLE

Like a limpet recording its fastidious journeys
I may never know the music of the world
but I can fathom time. This trail begun
through ten thousand neap tides, sees Amundsen,
a watcher of the pools, trace silver coils
rounded like earlobes listening for the footfalls.

Glimpsed as a prism on the radio telescope,
hauled like a bow on the raised strings of the bridge,
was that a change of pace or tone?
A wave or a particle? Or just the ice floes arguing?

I. Alma Again

JULY IN BETTYSTOWN

When the linen flaps open
with its east coast view of the Mournes,
and Ian Fleming novelettes
hide in a pile of fragrant clothes,

there is always the sea —
that reeling silence on a line,
and the clay like ground tarragon,
with its stench of burnished brine.

And always the hint of fire,
the thatch in its myriad parts,
and the air full of black-tailed grass
that sometimes has red hearts.

A CYCLE ON BETTYSTOWN STRAND

The nuns worked at their offices till noon
while on the strand I hummed a cycling tune.
And truth to tell, and on my own,
I rode the arc towards Mornington.
The nuns meanwhile in squat lean-tos
dreamt of milk and its residues,
quiet hearts till the evening sun
they shrieked down to the drifting foam,
in pirouettes childlike and humane
curious lives in an airy domain,
where one-piece black bathing suits
cradled skin in the habit of truth,
showing how silence goads technique
and heals the profane in a pathétique.

LAYTOWN RACES 1959

While searching for a place to land
my beloved aviator trails his voice
like a tea stain in the sky.

For he is running dry
across corrugated chalets, open fenlands
and a prairie of saline fields.

He wonders how far above the tidemark
we should stake out his course
while reeling in a line of stage fright

and, though the radio has no report of this,
I see the shy heat of the dunes,
the beach becoming crowded

and men strolling down Tiernan's Lane.
Why then should my mother say,
in thrall to the turning of the year—

he will come from the marsh road
past the links and the bawn?
For decked out in khaki

I'll soon be called to eat or swim.
The horses are held back with bunting.
A languorous tide is coming in.

ALMA AGAIN

My father has travelled down for the weekend.
He tiptoes from the scullery, yearning, I suppose,
for his smoky rooms where men exhale,
talking of horses, guineas, Redbreast
or the whiff of shag tobacco in an ox-tail.

His pipe snorts like a little pot stove
as he sneaks over the sleepers to the far bedroom.
Linen flaps in the rust-embroidered air.
End of July 1951, he comes into his own,
and I almost feel I am there.

Only my mother can say this wasn't true,
though, when she closes her eyes chanting vespers,
she reveals my snow-blind tattoo.

MY FATHER RETIRES LIKE TERRENCE MALICK

Nabokov's French doctor,
the one who said that in near relatives,
the faintest gastric gurgle
has the same 'voice',
scares me into the garden
to spray for codlin moth.

Not the bushy headed codlins for goldfinches
nor the smell of the leaves slightly bruised,
or the codlin hedge that secures a walk,

but the larva that feeds
on the kernels of apples and pears.
My father taught me when to spray,
using as an *aide-mémoire*
the drizzle smell of mildew,
and he armed me with a drenching gun
with its dead bouquet
of Jayes distemper leaking at the brim.

So while the moths laid their eggs
near the end of June
I would attempt to emulate
his feeble whistle tunes —

that one about the boll weevil, perhaps,
but more likely
I will be lying down and dreaming,
of those branchy locusts
coming with news
of their own Armageddon
out of the *Days of Heaven*.

SNOWSTORM

Snow all day, an eiderdown of wet clay
basking and banking, coming into land—

how many days since we left you
snug in your little basin underground?

The blank cold as you settled in
will be an erasure; dusting, muffling

as its echo and bounce
plumes like a broadcast—*son et lumière*—

in this extraordinary year start.
The few cars that waltz on bolts of lace

slalom on the kerb's incline
petitioning trees to embrace—

and I recall how Captain Scott's men
watched in awe a model of St. Paul's

float by in the Antarctic.
Such infelicities, such confusions,

as the phone inert in its cradle
starts to ring. A friend enquires of us,

the living alone and infirm,
'the pubs are still open, shall we adjourn?'

THE FIFTIES PARENT

When he smiled, Khrushchev hovered towards me,
airbrushing days with bliss,

and his bald baby's wrinkled face
was almost touching, almost miming a kiss.

II. THE QUAKER WALL

THE QUAKER WALL

The stuff from the hedgerow
I thought might be my laurel wreath,
we cut back one evening
near the end of July.

Honeysuckle, bramble, a nest of freesias,
and copper tubes
that whitened like bamboo,

all of which—muck and scree—
I forked and hauled
and over the Quaker wall I threw.

More like imaginary clay pots,
these uncovered manholes and drains
are gathered up to lie on these pages
until they can be rearranged.

DOUBTS NEAR COOSAN

We must have looked like a swimming stag,
head up, eyes in the dark
around Hare Island, around midnight.
We called for the monks in the little interior,
so little we could have made Borgesian copies
to roll like stitched or buttoned canvas
and pocket those lares of worship—
like the smiling garden Buddha, who holds aloft
a waterfont as a source for all the washes.

Though this was just an early morning skite—
the outboard opening its throat
to loft us round like a silly circumnavigation—
there is nothing to worry about.
Record it now, years later, a night out
to drink beer or its time might disappear.
Yet to come so far on a whim
and be caught fast in the breaking moon,
peering into the parallel lives
of our darling co-habitees,
we are so ignorant and arrogant to patronise
the night moves, the domestic shuffle of these.

MURPHY'S HEXAGON REVISITED
i.m. Patrick King

Ten years after our March race across Ireland to Omey,
Volkswagen replaced by a Renault, I visit the hexagon alone.
Through a stumbling graveyard, past a couple saving hay
in this wet summer's one God-given day.

Fifteen hands high it appears to stand,
like an old English thrupence weeping bronze into sand.
And though beguiled in its space—a dovetail net of mercy—
the sloped bed, stove and desk covet the margins of sea.

But who owns this washing line, these lazy-beds that curl,
the zigzag of hedging as the light bars unfurl?
And is this a right-of-way, did I walk across or drive,
is this the latitude, the one day the sea does not arrive?

THE BRIDEGROOM IN MOYCULLEN

On the day you were to be married there was a giddy air, and
I was asked to take you out, so the guests could stay clear
and gather their thoughts. With nothing in mind we drove,
turning right for the logical route down off the main road to
the lake, visible, shining and discreet, lying back in its thirsty
light. But when the road finally gave out and we had come
face up to a farmyard where four or five men were loading
sheep, or unloading as the case may be, it could have been a
backstreet on the lower side as some deal unravelled before
our eyes. I had to three-point the car back to the road of tar
and through a veil of flies and oaths, we left that morning
meeting of souls. The wedding party began in bright sun, un-
finished business, work to be done, and the evening passed
over unconcerned as though what brought us to these days
would be all we retain out of the land we erase.

SILENCE VISIBLE ON THE LOUGH INAGH ROAD

The few lodges are closed still
and the caretaker winter staff
burn the rubbish that accumulates
in some version of prior time.
Opening windows turn and turn about,
they check paint lines,
while that skitter of anti-fowling
fondles the tied-up lake boats.
Things occur, almost without cause,
or in a dust waltzing as it falls
raised pontoons rake the lazy water,
a plateau of derricks slithers on guys
of steel, while archipelagos of sound,
those cries in slipshod time,
are the stuff of intrigue,
yet to be revealed.

NORTH/WEST

Making off for our autumn break
we stumble through the B&Bs of Leitrim and Sligo.
At breakfast there is the shredding fax
someone's reservations about the weather
turning to tickertape perhaps.
But these tandem falls
bring us to the Villa Nova in Drumcliff
or the Benjamin Franklin in Drumahaire.
And when our car idles
in some grassy *leataobh*
I watch Mr. Kaplin check out
of the Plaza Hotel in New York
en route to the Sheridan Johnson
in Rapid City, South Dakota.

Such confusions arise
in taking on a job that might become your life,
so if this were crop-dusting time
we might be in danger.
But the weather outside is rainy
and the fields are neat
in their black plastic dresses,
as if we had worked all summer
to get to this. So hold out your hand
and lift me onto the forehead of stones
where pollen speckles our skin,
while in the ghost of a copper rinse
that magnesium smell
of October rambles in.

ABOUT ABSTRACTION

No more unusual are the salmon smolts.
They flee Killary, sprouting wings,
in a droning helicopter out of their element
into the weightlessness of things.

MOVING INTO ST. VINCENT'S PARK

In the space that is always new
I check the joists for sleepwalking,
the cornices for collisions,

and the wired abstractions
for the buoyancy of emissions.
Though the keel is battened and spliced,

and the upturned bar
rocks on its stanchioned coasters,
I wait like a beaded bowl

for that mythical riptide.
But where are the owners of each silhouette,
whose dreams and affections are gone,

when in the wonder that still remains
with all the Pole's realignments,
my window faces its same threequarters—

that glinting parabola of light
like the battery cell of a lost comet,
swimming far in the zones out there?

DUSK WALKS

We walk the same route every night
trying to fathom the small debris of cars—
how coils, springs, sprockets and rings
dither in a tired samba,
until scuffed along pavements and gutters.
On the West Pier tufts of wild wheat
spear up in a jaunty confident air—
what do we think we are doing here:
hopelessly colonizing like these foolish seeds
or walking off excess and fear?

As the mailboat breathes its drift of sooty snow
a bushel of love on spread arms
wheels from its flaky undertow,
and dreaming there on plashing lines
garrulous eyes and shy lights
wink back seeming to say—
the noise of the world is so terrible
we can endure it only
by being coated with drowse.

SHINGLES

This is a peppercorn deal
        with trembling late snags,
                a fault line fracture

with insincere blight,
        a bubble settling itself
                splayed on the electric field,

a tripswitch that failed to ignite.
        As though a surface, all noise
                could be rude with the world

and would inevitably dissipate—
        a turlough, a name only,
                lapsing in a thrill of dissonance

while the music of its drone
        chatters away in a shin dance.
                So we shiver and demur

as if this rush for a cure
        could entice the dormant plagues
                and all their little retinues.

CLARE HOUSE

We are rocking on a frozen bed,
prow, like a Boyne Coracle
oars upended, held fast,
and we tense our stomachs
to let each other pass.

A barge or yacht might break free,
but we have tons of oak
and underneath the snarl
of telegraph and telephone.

PAPIER-MÂCHÉ

In school we raised our world
on a script of papier-mâché,
mountains folded on the legal notes,
rivers embraced the steady downpour
and winter fields floated off unread.
So my aquatic-veined preliminary maps,
arbitrary and self-important,
might just have got it right!

Today the charts of ice and snow
bleat and punctuate a different lie.
They speak of the occasional music of rain,
the percentages when navigating unmanned
as though my new répétiteur should play
with the morse of the Benny Goodman band.

REHEARSING BECKETT

Beckett walked the East Pier
to plead with Neptune, to entreat —

and McGovern like MacGowran
now mouths the words
on his cellular, mid-week,
mid-winter, Hejira.

Is this what it means to be
anointed, unexamined,
a tattler on the West Pier
without a thought or a care,
and oblivious of the furies
roused by the pilot light
of my solitary Disque Bleu?

APRIL 1963

At the end of December with the sky dark and full
Bud Powell creates the hyphen for Dexter Gordon
in *Willow Weep for Me.* Some encouraging voice
has its moonlit brocade filtered down
as the session's altimeter prints the air of Paris 1963.

I have forgotten my classroom and Glenn Gould's silent holler.
You could forget everything when days are filled
with notes like these, the tempo of fahrenheit and centigrade,
the composition of oil on frieze, though it might yet snow,
and in the morning the little footprints will be
quavers surfacing through the undertow.

ART PEPPER REMEMBERS PAUL DESMOND

The way the air shifts you would think
there was no medium out there—

all notes cut from the flame of ice
will cherish the blow-by-blow I scare
into the vacuum that is already gone.

And there is no accounting for this,
what we walk and talk in
is essentially humbling and flattering,

though what it all commands
is this somnambulant line
clouding the issue with its beat and its time.

I am riding down through smoke and vapour,
trying to remember not the air itself,
but this air, this lithe composure of song—

how the disparate necklace of plucks and beats
could challenge the dissonance of wrong.

ST. STEPHEN'S DAY

After the church service
we park beside the cemetery
waiting for the drenched mourners
to pass by.

Leading us in trenchcoats,
they resemble the break-up continuity
of that civil war film,
and we, the peripheral characters

smirking in the almost out-of-shot.
Though we may genuflect
and catch the squalls
trailing their five minute lulls of blue,

we take this chance
to stand and listen
to the bleached white epiphanies
and the little offices

where space conceives infinite space
and breviary translates into missal.
So stand clear
on this St. Stephen's Day

at the edge of one version of events,
where our thinning shadows
count the hours
of the pale immaculate sun,

but fail to retrieve
the picnic sites
from Kinnegad to Kilcock,
the truck stops on Route 66.

LEAVING SAINT HELEN'S

The swarm of black-clad novices
walking past our door
in groups of three

vanished overnight.
Now as fields
fill with rape

and the perfumed garden
reverts to pasture,
the great house resembles

an impromptu barracks.
A world is being
mobilised or demobbed,

doors flung open,
moon-dazed clocks
running fast,

and, like sappers
lost in the North Wood,
we lean to the right

feeling for balance
while the earth drags
beneath our feet.

Time is moving away.
It happens like that.
People lose interest.

THE ERNE WATERS

If Ireland holds with Mercator's cruel web
I think tonight of the Ballinamore Canal—
the smart-card hydraulics, a love unto itself.

But should the locks become undone,
that wine-dark cargo, that wonderful weeping chaos,
might tip like a snagged gutter

on our makeshift pelmet of clip and anchor,
to feed the gravel bins, basins and pots
while we pan for the glittering aurora dust.

SKETCHING STILLBIRTH

The femerell with its louvre
        and string of smoke,
the callows and that fatigue
        they call on.

The pipit's drone,
        the bushes of artichoke,
the windowless dorm
        smelling of eiderdown.

QUINSY

Imagining I had quinsy
I gave the grass a quiff
where it was turning to meadow.

But just as a fever
curls in its own smoke
I found it hard to swallow,

that a guillemot
blown off course
could succumb to rumour,

or eyeing Sweet William
in my thatch of garden,
come down on the side of caution.

And I could be his nemesis,
his thorn, his briar,
though I could as well

resemble the red kite
ghosting a saraband
through the Coto Doñana,

as I know my nurse
who tethers the spatula
will tease the cipherings

of bile and sand,
while we search for the kiss,
the signature, the error.

MOUTH MUSIC

It shouldn't come down
to anything so crude
as the stone at Blarney.

But it was you who said
that kissing its runic lines
with legs agape

might lead to talk of farney,
or so I mumbled
as we took the floor,

the band striking up
a salty Cajun score—
and though I have stumbled

through the grace notes
strewn amongst
Brendan Behan's patois,

I trace my craving
back to the slime left
on our plate of rue and blather.

Note:
The Letters of John Cheever (Jonathan Cape, 1989), page 228. Brendan Behan: 'Now that
I'm off the sauce I'm much more interested in farney'. 'What is farney' asked Mrs. Vanderlip.
'Farney, mam', said Behan, 'is an abbreviation for farnication'.

CROP CIRCLES

Optics swam as it pawed and stretched
before coming to, with tiny fists clenched.
Somehow that spirit never stayed clear
when we sent it to London for its little acid bath,
but on the green baize of Crumlin
we idly traced its smooth belly and groin.

Now in a foolish way, as it pines
for a bed of cloves, a den of mulch and carbon
we see it as a rogue sign
to stretch the fields of turpentine,
an impression of tallow in an inky duress
to tuck and pin these shipping lanes,
these freshly dug canals,
like a spinning thurible of excess.

A RED CITY JOURNAL

*

Like an addendum we thought to emerge from geography
into the slim ventricle of Via Dante—
a windbreak or a firebreak, a breather
before the goldrush of another summer.

*

But further into the addendum, a snow-blind quietens
the swagger of the time-track
and some ethylation gathers force—
annex, colonnade, or a dream of bones,
as we rinse our oil and gel
with the stout bottle of angostura bitters.

*

Lost in the warp and flutter of the portico,
creeping past that abandonment,
is a space for the less divine
who would never confuse an ox-tail
with the beaded stump of a pig's trotter,
but might incline to fecklessness
or use a tea-stain to establish veneration,
or think the space that plumes on high
is tethered to the swing of a metronome.

*

I could now open De Sica's parentheses
and in that studious arbor
line-up time, blow circles,
and prepare to stand outside myself.

But we embrace the armada of semiotic smells,
studded almond and coriander,
powders like the silk of perfume
spread-eagled in their tall bins,
while *The Garden of the Finzi-Continis,*
its vanished, decaying, melancholy glamour,
is every closed door
guarding the parallel calm of absolution.

*

At the Porta Barricana, a pilgrim halt,
a familiar largesse becomes a further incidental—
a tree space, a breather, a chapel of ease,
just as the running track of our tram
on the enamel of the bled stones
improvises tide-lines as contrails
to mimic the nave of the sky.

*

From the cold of the Apennines
come rain and its calamities—
benevolent spring bells, spattering leaky chimes,
the stench of mallow, eucalyptus and pine.

These basketfuls of sodden air are a siphoning
for the finches as we walk down Via Augusto Murri,
and as though in a forest
the sky echo drums on our fontanelles.

*

The phone machine takes all the messages,
outside a yardman burns March leaves,
while the woman overhead

plays skittles in shoes with high heels.
you lie feverish in your cot—
my mother or my daughter—
and your side table has expectorant, powder tots,
and drugged sleep's burnt magenta.

*

To a pension on Via Drapperie,
once a two-hour rooming house.

The taxi driver smirks as he gathers our bags.
Surgical room, like post theatre,
tiled floor, raftered ceiling painted white,
wardrobe, writing desk, fake chandelier,
an old radiator, quiet—

what are these signatures that cannot be undone?
We guard our language like a foreign tongue.

*

Our last look at Neptune, mocking the photomontage
of resistance in this red city.
One small postcard print has a man hanging forward,
dead standing at his shooting post—
his working smock belies a petulant ghost.
Retreating down that silhouette
of inky grains and dots,
I steer toward the catacombs
where painted heatpipes yawn and cough.
And groaning like a ship at sea,
adrift in the balm of a eucharistic night
we empty the bilges in the marine pantry.

SHE SCRATCHES HIS WRIST

She scratches his wrist once or twice
they tell in signals of their private vice.

I am a witness, not some eye from above
some things we do not know, or only tell in love.

PRINTING THE LEGEND

The train journey into Venice
pulls across the morning swamp,
through what one painter might hold
was turmoil, written into grains and pigments—
or so our host retold.

In Ford's *The Man Who Shot
Liberty Valance* there is a similar
black-and-white chamber
of dots and smoke
where a train parts the prairie
like a mink admiring its coat.

These are false starts, like a false dawn,
but how else could Ford,
or Fellini in *Amarcord,*
begin to print the legend
except to say, the lead story
in today's *Shinbone Star*
tells of who is the toughest man
south of the Picketwire.

HOMAGE TO GEORGE ELIOT IN NEW HAMPSHIRE

Twenty-two years or more
and I transplant the twenty-two volume
complete works of George Eliot
up to my little attic store,
which now takes in the panorama
of the Quaker graveyard
none greater than its neighbour.

As we settle in, I recall
how I gathered autumn fruit,
driving through Bethlehem, Medicine Falls,
sober villages on a Greyhound's morning suit.
And dreaming of that past,
Eliot on her shelf, I come up for air
in the arms of my own self.

WORKING FOR THE GOVERNMENT

Walking these cut-throat fields
far from the latest outrage,
my thin-lipped parchments
show the short, sharp inlets
where the Atlantic blares.
In the drone and swathe of meetings
we tell how money allocates,
how long corridors
stretch into the lime of mid-evening
and how chimes rise and bathe
like a submerged village of commerce
hanging onto the edge of the world.
Now we have only distance—
documents on deal tables,
a feathery importance mumbling
incoherences, as here in Easter Week
I rewrite the cloven, haphazard
labyrinth of the order of my life.
Hardly the stuff of obituaries!

LENTEN OFFERING

Though we have nothing to show
for all our talk of drizzle, colcannon,
and a glossary of moss,
on St. Patrick's Day in Bologna
we unwrap our *living shamrock*
ready to wear, conceived near
the monastic settlement of Skellig Rock.

But it refuses to reveal itself,
or to set sail in its vial of tepid water;
like a mauve lily
unimpressed to be roused so soon,
its belly shows off a spray of liver spots,
confusing seepage with a tang
of cancerous vermouth. Undaunted,
I prepare the mock silver paten
and bless the little tangle
as if we were back in our bedroom,
out of time, saying mass.

Water & Power

PART ONE

OFFERING THE LIGHT

If three white on the scoreboard
should lead to an offer
to abandon the day's endeavour,
I'll play the night watchman

who heads for the pavilion
taking for company
a last glance round silly point,
a brief sweep of boundary and bye

and one more entry
for that loose archive, .
where the real map of Dublin
is about the same size as Dublin.

A CAROL FOR CLARE

whisper your name in Phibsboro
through prison yard and hospital

tiptoe through Portobello
assembling choir and canticle

pass on the grain of Rialto
where fog and snow are audible

still the hours in Pimlico
harmonise a madrigal

lie with your ghost in Marino
shepherd the final decibel

MENZIES' FIELD

The first sun of the year
clips the spongy red trunks
of the redwoods,
as I sniff the Pacific air
that Menzies,

ship surgeon on the Vancouver expedition,
quaffed two hundred years ago.
St. Patrick's Eve,
give or take a decade,
the ground like a trampoline,

I am up to my neck in resin
and my goitre throat
stinks of gum,
recording last year's triumphs
like the painted cemeteries

of Audubon.
Even the smallest flight
is here preserved,
though the wing beat
and the throat song

are less revered.
As I play your new year tape,
sweet nothings from The Grateful Dead,
I hear that Menzies,
perhaps to fend off scurvy,

told his ancestors
to turn their backs on the sea
and when they knelt down
with my quiet uncles,
they grew an island of barley.

TRAIL

On Prince Edward Island
a moose regards what lies before him
with the resignation
of what he left behind
near Ballynahinch Lake
all those years ago.

Lifting his head, he fears the rumour
that betrays how calls uttered
on the high valleys of the Maumturks
are never erased.

They echo on the ocean floor
when the fibre-optic cable,
anxious to record it all,
fidgets and snags.

CHARACTER IN SEARCH OF AN AUTHOR

Along the wide boulevard of ships and sheds,
dry docks, cranes, riggers, marine railways,
there is a serpentine, salt-caked house
where bramble, fuchsia,
honeysuckle and heavy vine
have crept out of my control.

Should my heart give out
and I am left on this porch to watch,
this will all slide into wilderness
and as I lay aside my espadrilles,
the panicked wren fleeing a patch of salal
is there to remind me, that I know
the date of my birth, but don't yet know
the date of my death, and never shall.

TEEPEE AT BOW LAKE

Teepee at Bow Lake, Medicine Hat, Alberta
July 10, the man looking towards Eden
has his mind set on the spiralling cost
of his film set, soon to be called *Heaven's Gate*.

THE RAILWAY GUARD

Past the church, a brambled lane,
the remains of dairy farms,
legal notes hammered onto fence posts
and fields of assorted grasses
burning clear to the iron track.

Out of this dry clay near Gormanston,
in the needle-white of November,
men still bring their horses down
to hug the foreshore
as if what they fear in the encroaching tide
is not the tide alone.

Moon worshippers used to winter here,
and their bitumen chalets,
in vapours of creosote,
now lie chalked-pegged for the Geiger boys
so all our bruised affection
bristles in cardoons and docks.

From such marine enamel,
sandy scores of the black and the white
might tell how we recede
in the scant world
of the bled photogravure,
but Clare smiles and whispers
that here is as good as anywhere
to mimic the salmon shoals
who never betray
what gossip might thrive
in the olive orchards and seaweed barrios.

I know that fifteen summers
spent on my knees, combing through
eel grass, sea holly, sea lavender,
could never hope to appease,
but when she walks to greet
my grandfather – the railway guard –
on his Marsh Road settee,
she is whiter than all of these.

LUDWIG, RUTH & I

Gathered on your verandah we drink and talk
about neighbours in a found land. You brought
Susanna Moodie's clarity, settled in Victoria's air
but never spoke of that albino shack at Cape Spear.
Its charcoal heart on your landing now
beseeches the children to come home, safe and sound.

In this street of maple quarter lots
built for the plain man in the early 1900s,
your next-door neighbour
has summoned the municipal inspector
to translate a template of roods and perches,
to admonish the laburnum when it overreaches,
so that, in another time and far from home
when we unspool the fences, language alone
might lasso the blond interior or confuse
the world we live in with the words we use.

LOOKING UP

Hanging washing on the line,
September scudding winds abating,
that whole other world of fleece
looks down on these allotments.

Just like that migrant soul
I saw in the Okanagan,
and her string of palominos —
she too was looking up.

THE WARDS

After the final blizzard I found her head
lying amongst the strings of the tent.

Those ribbons of longitude might have hidden
in their sickle cells the spine of a parachute,

though no breeze told more of what
she had come through than all these wires

humming their silent arias.
In the scattered sacristies the dead

will be praying with oak-dark hands,
and stroking her forehead, I fear

the seahorse in her thinning hair
will be all that remains of the fluted sealskin

embroidered with the scare of bones
as ornaments. The cubicle awning billows,

a mailchute for the rogue train
and we carry the vase of her baby breath

whispering psalms in a dutiful refrain:
Tower of Ivory, brave souls on the run,

unfathomable gestures for King Harvest
who has surely come.

FIRST FRIDAYS

I will follow her with pen and wash
investing braziers to suck and puff
a last gasp from the hurried Westerlies.
Recording beads with halts and stations,
on her own carvings, her own intonations,
she'll pause in her time as a chatelaine,
and if the Bowery man who might be her brother,
passes on the street, in love with no other,
she'll emerge at Christchurch
to launch a last assault on good fortune,
mumbling truths crammed in a missal womb,
as though memorial cards could be more than
paper-folded invocations of how
and when we should plead, and to whom.

I CANNOT STAY

When Swift succumbed to Meniere's
he began to finger cuffs of cloth
making a swooned arc with fabrics

as if he had found that one forgotten piece.
On her daily spin round the frosty beds,
looking for a sense of balance, I tell her

that the treble in her inner ear
might be Euclidean voices trying to appease
the arc of a prolonged circus striptease.

And though she drags all of this, or her version of this,
to the grave, she hasn't yet climbed
the steps to the gates of her dotage.

STONEY ROAD

Tell me once more what she said as she lay
on the polished bed of anthracite, cool to the touch –
you'll pray that I am taken from this house, one day –
as if words alone could ask for so much.

THE WATCHERS' HOUSE

A nut-black swallow on the verandah
struggles to pen her ruminant Alhambra,

gathering a pelmet above the lintel
with gentle spires of mud and spittle.

*

Perhaps she fears an unfinished mosaic
could rouse the shadows crowding the gate,

but two by two like a Watchtower militia
when we follow down in our famine regalia

*

may she fly over the whole elation
that rides to our piebald hut,

so we can taste resignation
in her reluctant backward look.

PRAYERS AT THE COAL QUAY

The spine of the *Leinster*
pipes its basso continuo,
its triple note linear fugue,

and, with flexed sirens,
turns in its own length
prompting a slight recoil

where lazy barques nuzzle hulls,
windsurfers crouch in the swell
and all the walkers breaking stride,

pause and check their midday bell.
In this sweet communion
within earshot of the next drowning,

mailboats yawn or come about,
taking stock of wind and light,
and like us, list to port

at exact extremes of home,
dreaming a world of meridians,
purlins for Cancer and Capricorn.

FROM PORTSTEWART TO PORTRUSH

A biplane rumbles like a tractor in the sky
looking for its field, its crops to spray,
or confusing a scribble with reverie
for that speckled egg and muffled cry.

But perhaps it's searching for all that remains
of whistles and hoots from driverless trains,
dissolving dreams and all that entails,
or the debt to pleasure in the mundane.

THE STONE HOUSE: DROMOD HARBOUR

Boat piers are much alike.
Stepping ashore at The Stone House,
doused in the inky stream of Acres Lake

we walk a tarmacadam line
where curvature comes together
as strands of carmine

climb through migrant sprays
of laburnum and maple.
In a wait that slowly accumulates

until too long, hours refract,
and like a tiptoeing through a glass lean-to
we examine the stills of this romance—

the trays of alpines dusted over,
the hunter's shot leaving no report,
the tennis court going under—

trying to fathom that flinty allure
as somehow the wail
of the long-haul Dublin train

recalls a man who was falling,
crying out somewhere
for his coffee-stained hill,

folding his wings as if all he desired,
was a polished strip
amongst petrified pines,

where the stain of silence
would be heaven sent,
and boat piers would greet the innocent.

MANSION HOUSE WARD

The guide says, moth-gold,
a sulphur beard,
happy to repeat faded nectarine,
happy to embrace one word
and so be sure of its origin.

In any event—
an ancient red dust,
carried as ballast,
pilfered and canonised,
rising up,
brick by brick
for the shelter of houses
will for now, more than our speech,
define these parts.

THE DRUID'S CLOAK

They say he was only one of three
to grasp Einstein's theory of relativity.

They say he married the footprints on his blackboard
with the compromises and the promises

and the erratic haphazard
over the half-door of his glasses.

They say he knew the stony fields of ogham
like etchings on an earwig's backpack,

and, as if to fathom
the chirp of the microchip,

they say he knew their filigreed circuits
in the memory of jaunts.

So if he still admired the standing still,
that flush on a parallel line

should be enough to chase him down
the miniature world of the paradigm.

LIKE STONEHOUSE

We were completing the last bank of the dam
when he appeared and waved down
to my sister playing tennis on the strand.
Driving from the heat of St. Stephen's Green
he made claim to our here and now
though his swaddled Vaseline gave off that acrid fear
known also to Sergeant Troy and Paul Revere.

Strolling to the water, he made to cross over,
and though he had five thousand days in store,
he was assembling the route of departure.
Now, when we lay down our little bundle
like a goalpost or an umpire's chair,
he urges us to strike out in a languid freestyle,
make it up as you go along.

EVERYTHING IN ITS PLACE

I glance down the windy canyons
where all the metals flow
and an American Indian
shinnies up a column of steel
retrieving core samples from far below.
Settling the rods
he follows his pit-helmet's gaze
and, in a moment or so,
a beam comes floating towards him,
making so easily
it barely ruffles the undertow.
He might be one of the high-steeled Iroquois
composing a mute score
while pursuing the hint of snow
found only in his forebear's air.
I stare through double glazing,
hugging my indoor vertigo,
and he taps for sweet air
as though in baby semaphore
a silent major chord could show
that melody we all revere.

THE TAN SPIRALS

The tan spirals on the lawn
must come from the Quaker trees,
more in late spring they fall
and more numerous than the leaves.

Their song is like a faint cry,
that first ache in the rogue cell,
as though memory could ever justify
all we had yet to tell.

THE CANCER BUREAU

The nurse paints on my puffed belly
the load line or the plimsol mark.
She says it will rise and fall through salt water
and, where tidal streams
connive to build their rudimentary dreams,
she says my weight will be greater.
So much for the spindles, pulleys and shafts
conspiring to show
my maximum permitted loading
for Winter North Atlantic, Indian Summer
and Tropical Fresh Water,
for, as I tell her over and over,
I never plan to leave this world again.

SEARCHING FOR PAUL HENRY'S SKY

If the opening shot of such a small bed
of timber frames set down on the flats
confirms what Lewis and Clark had said

what could be missing from our pleading?
Neat New England spires with those
tree-lined canals, settlement succeeding

settlement across miles of brush,
vetch embroidered ha-has replacing wires,
and pockmarked demesne houses

outlining new towns with acqueducts
and swamplands leading onto vine.
So should I wake and speak in tongues

or join the light-horsemen whose cries and calls
echo in blooms of frost, as saltpetre
or turf-banks prop up their gable walls?

Or should I plant a copse in memory of some
forgotten skirmish, a tease for a lone balloonist
to gaze on as he succumbs

like all of us here ready to incline
rather than erase the god
who sleeps in the dream of a paradigm?

I'll settle for the off-white in regret,
the blue that lies in Cashel Blue,
and clouds strung tight to a lariat.

MOVING A GARDEN SHED

We hauled the garden shed on rolling batons
up and over the split-level, trees uprooted,
timbers groaning, blood pumping like a church organ,
as though it were our dream to stall time,
bring back the silk of snatched music.

On the hottest day of the year
Fitzcarraldo's choirs came to bathe us.

QUINCE

For my new year resolution
I'll plant quince

in the boggy warren of the garden,
or in pots, trailing somewhat

but giving up their fat, like pears.
I'll spend autumn sniffing

the peachy down, on their soft baby heads,
place them in a bowl for pomander,

then scrape what fragrance comes
from the puckered leaves

to rub on my nonexistent spleen.
I may need a cure for dropsy,

a balm for the asthmatic lung,
something to place on the red

that inflames my eyes,
but, as forbidden fruit takes on

the fulsome curve of a dwarf cello,
I'll remain in the suit

of the man who flits
from roulade to madeleine,

conversant with all faiths
and believing in none.

WATER AND POWER

My father's watch
was the only thing I wore
when I dived into the Merrimack
in the summer of 1974.

An engagement present—
it seized with rust
faster than I could grapple
with the ties of trust.

I had let slip the role
that love plays
in a sketch or a rectangle,
and, though it had some way

to tease the future,
I was unaware
of such swift currents,
nor could I dare

to travel too far out
toward the wooden pins
following their line
in the racing mill.

Even if I could jump
into the same river twice,
so the watch could regain
what it was once,

how can I mourn a proof
for shock and dust
when water and power
are what needs must?

WIDE OF THE MARK

I know I should prefer
the busy conflagration
of reading through chain mail,

the tickertape of frightened stock
that utters from the weathervane,
something about that moment

when a star is in the east
as a slack-jawed anchorman
or a forgotten cosmonaut

omits to emphasise
that now is too late to spray,
or the premonition – call it intuition –

that this is all by the way,
even as my nurse
is coaxing a mirror

down the lining of my oesophagus,
pointing like an idiot savant
to the very heart of things.

ASYLUM HARBOUR

for the workers who built Dún Laoghaire Harbour

When I hauled myself up on our roof
   to settle a silver-speared cowl,
   your arms and my arms aligned
with Pigeon House, Baily and Kish.

   And as for that refuge, I recall
   a funicular with its mercury tilt,
ribbons of brine on a tattered hull,
   stone men singing shanty songs.

And if their wagons of Dalkey stone
are all preserved in this box of light,
   the sonar of dying ships
   the sirens in faded livery
are in every block that groans and strains
   as foghorns plead with memory.

PART TWO

CANOWER SOUND
for John & Kaye

A day so full of autumn
I am listening to the rustle of dead leaves.

*

Driving down to Recess
I enter the silence of Monument Valley.

*

Reversing from a steel gate,
through a wash of alders, at a snail's pace.

*

Again and again the morse of repairs,
bones chattering in some oratory.

*

For years, the same pile of blocks
strewn on the verge like unread books.

*

I log the stern reflection of an iceberg's stomach
as it prays for frost.

*

Our shore house lies back
dreaming of the white-washed coves of Venice.

*

Pre-terminal days, ghost derricks
are gathering on the Porcupine.

*

I stumble through our Boboli Gardens,
ruins, title deeds, quills.

*

Surrounded by the Latin names for flowers,
I am wading through a pharmacy of ills and cures.

*

Wild strawberries, cries and whispers
Samuel Barber's *Adagio for Strings*.

*

The small harbour wall wears brown kelp
at low tide, ten feet tall.

*

Where the ophthalmic inspector has retired,
fuchsia and iris thrive.

*

The dowager's house breathes onto a vacant lot—
the *Four Last Songs* with Lucia Popp.

*

The stone fields of Newfoundland—
Lindbergh peered down on these stone fields.

*

I pocket the clavichord of a thrush,
its afterthought, its wiry scale struck dumb.

*

Like a tuning fork, or just after—
I log the grey heron, our version of the crane.

*

Four púcáns waiting for the tide,
tethered like dray horses, side by side.

*

Passing over without a second glance,
a boll weevil, prophet of circumstance.

*

I cup an ear to the drone across the inlet—
the trigonometry of stones.

*

Long shadows in Cashel Hotel,
de Valera, de Gaulle, a brace of tall men.

*

Carrying seaweed in a samovar,
Jack Elam enters Boulger's Bar.

*

Bog cotton threading the verges
may tempt me from the path to browse.

*

Between our fens and dust bowl,
some ore we have yet to value
drowses underfoot.

*

And no lost domain, though a petulant wind
choreographs our need to remain.

*

A schooner out of Puget Sound
combs indentations round Bertraghboy.

*

From oubliette, from columbine,
a wind plays 'long fetch' to the waterline.

*

Intaglio men are burning gorse,
their pall of smoke like heaven scent.

*

Our tide comes and goes
murmuring in the shag and slime of stones.

*

A neighbour in the evening checking lobster pots
might be seeking his mythical point.

*

Burren Greens in thrall with the light,
yet they only seem to come on at night.

*

Seal pups feed on the ebb tide—
midges, sprats and flies.

*

Waves dance ashore arm in arm
like a couple of swells.

*

The radio's apologetic tone,
the weatherman's take on mezzotint,
cold fronts burn like sorrel in stone.

*

Now that everyone is gone,
nothing interrupts silence
except a goat's song.

*

At the hour of the wolf I improvise
a singing line for Bix and Ives.

*

We find our light in escrow,
alcohol, alkaline,
stars strung out like stillborn snow.

*

As night's sky reclaims the headland,
ruined house by ruined house
ascends into a heaven of sorts.

*

I sleep on Bergman's ivory shore,
take auburn light from his belvedere.

*

Another day full of autumn
sees the kitchen garden putting on new leaves.

from *Hombre: New and Selected Poems*

STILL MAN

The sum of what I see or believe
is simply the case, or mostly true,
and if the limits of my experience
set bounds on the way the world is,
at least for me, no doubt rivers
will soldier on even as I sleep
and fail to keep vigil at their bridges.
The truth that I am wreathed in error
allows me to retreat through the fallacy
of laws in language and broach the matter
that I am here, composing the compass
of worth, while remaining the god
of my own importance, often listless,
often singing out like Chanticleer.

A LOVE STORY

Last night we camped
on Boss Croker's acres,
tonight we cross
a river in spate,

in the miles between
a white-haired man
carries his gospel of brake-
pads and corrugated iron

like the sheets of asbestos
which we found to our cost
when we tramped
through Kippure and Ticknock.

We cough in unison,
we argue over direction
and though we had come
in search of Rue des Favorites,

to take on the lowdown
of its honky-tonk bars,
we bear witness to unnamed
toxins, the domestique

who gestures like a friend,
as the halting ambition
that dithers and skews
and is brought to its knees

lets us gaze again
on brownfield and edgeland
with all the aplomb
of Mir's captain.

AN OLD BOYNE FISH BARN

You should have seen the sea in those days,
wind smoke and weeping flares washing

ashore from the barrios, all those
hesitant evacuees, as tarpaulin stretched

along Beaufort's Dyke and our drift nets
sailed through the Hebrides. Shuffling in pipe

smoke, scribbling a plume of grave longing
on the bones of a wax-bright dusk,

I stood to see the ranks at the fish barn –
open mouthed, open boxed, iced on shelf

after shelf – and stayed to inhabit
what remains for the solipsistic raconteur

who believes the weight of his vision
will dissolve with his last sigh. When I drag

a heavy catch out of the evening,
old weather, braced for meteorites,

groans like a dehumidifier and burbles
the gospel of faith and love and water.

FRANK

When they dismantled the spokes of the union,
slowly but surely songlines appeared in the forest
and our charts had no more call
for the watchtowers and wire curtains
or the ready army of reserve
rusting in a century-old slumber.

And, just as in deep time we are slowly
but surely drifting from the equator,
and know less of how and when
the harrier should side with the hen,
you paused so your footfalls
could lightly strum the surges in flood water,
the banks of purple loosestrife, as you knelt
to anoint the anonymous and peripheral.

FROST MOVING

In the long days between the anniversaries
of Little Bighorn and Bloomsday
what passes for the sun in these parts

beats down on the living and the dead.
A Santa Clara man
checks out of Finn's Hotel

and, just as it was
one hundred years ago to the day,
he seems to know something

we don't know. Wearing a kerchief
of dried tobacco leaves
tied loose on his throat,

braided hair like a tennis player
and the white profile badge of FDR,
he says we are all being assimilated

into the one race and, however far-fetched,
our smiles are coming together.
So when I check into Finn's Hotel

I stroke my yellow hair
and the maid in love with dew on the lens
carries my bags up a winding stair.

IN MY READING

If there is such a thing anymore
as a humble servant in the vineyard

this is he, a man from the coast
home on his lunch break,

working the stooped enclosure
below me as I read and revel

in the feral words of murder
on what passes for a roof garden

with a view of Pompeii,
and further below

through French doors,
you sleeping, an afternoon to dream

or pray after the heat of love making,
just as his turning broken clay

with a method learned as a boy
becomes a kind of recreation

to justify and while away
olive baskets filled with autumn

as his mother, who once
combed her hair like Myrna Loy,

watches with approval
this noise of renewal

or so it appears
in my reading.

22/09/07

I pull onto the hard shoulder
one hundred miles from anywhere,
and, if I have mislaid sleep,
tonight or tomorrow will be
one hundred years since his burbles
and sobs reached out in the chill
of a Drogheda bedroom, a lying-in.

And from a womb that was snug and serene
or tight as a drum, to this night talk,
creeping fog and traffic scum,
or the panic left in the maw
of a feline papoose—
he has me set for the surf of the day,
will o' the wisp, footloose.

HEAD THE BALL

Next to last page
black and white
Seurat pigments
sideburned figures
emerge from a fog
that could be from
another century
and is,
while the freezing
germ of attempted sleet
vies with the balletic
abandon
of a glancing header
resembling
a polished cue ball
either or both
bereft of a full
Bobby Charlton.
The lines down
to a bullet of text,
record the fast
forward –
a scout's eye,
a franchise for
aluminium sidings,
sharp suits on
a motor lot,
or too early
fought that brave fight.
And the legend
speaks through every
blustery Saturday

when nip
meant tuck,
and heads like
imperial eggs
were sleek
as Fabergé.

LOW TIDE

To get to the riverbed
and then the rivermouth
we must wade through

a heat that thrives
under the living railway arch,
past a factory compound,

the half-hearted tarmac
of a starter estate
and the bails of wire mesh

rolled on a midden
for that once-in-a-generation
floodplain. We'll pass

a school of outreach mummers
and, nearer the sea,
locals with billycans

of lugworms and maggots.
And we come, mere functionaries,
to check a minor river

and its tributaries, to count
palisades as mooring posts,
and, before the estuary can fill again,

make of this counting
a file of contention,
like the life cycle

of gypsy moths,
like the stories that fade
along excavated pots.

MAGAZINE

I don't believe a word
of her silent stare,
in a lock-up
on a ruined lot
where the bath in the corner
is caked with blood.
She may have come
from far flung Duleek
for this tired tableau,
but in the pewter light
of a vague afternoon,
indifference freighted with script,
she is somehow reduced
from a ragged tribe,
wearing the goodbye look,
as a given text
falls into font after font.
So take finger stain,
hair and saliva,
check the breech
in the magazine,
gather swabs to assuage
some breathless profile,
and then bring vials
into the teeming street
where anonymity is comfort,
silence is its own reward
and shrift turns up
singing its mad song.

NO GOING BACK

Although there is no going back
this one has taken for the road.
With about half his life still to go,
he gets up from the garden bench,
unleashes the halts that bind him
to his first-born son
and exits by the long back field
with pocket watch, clip and sounding line,
signatures that have gone
as some way to talk about oblivion.
He will make for the beaches of north Dublin,
the sandy fields that mark the border
with Meath, and carry on
until the sounds for Louth become insistent,
until he can flag down
something of the spirit that we leave
behind and always seek to recall,
though where this leaves me—
a moment of elation or tardy withdrawal
years hence—is anyone's guess.

TOSS

Every year they come together
like the risen sap of bamboo,
crosscut canes pitch and toss,
all the families waving, in the blossom-
laden branches of the pear trees.

Hives that once sang like choirs
lie against the gable walls
of their churches and schools,
tossed in the dust of quarantine
like old tea chests, apothecaries' desks.

They are praying, you see, with their
legs and arms coated in pollen,
that these fleeting caresses can give
hope to the smocks and dresses that live
as a ripening swell in the blossom.

PRESTON'S

Like the stout Dimple Haig
filled with old English sixpences,

shot-packed goitre for a snipe's neck,
a last bottle of Preston's

lay on the false bottom of a chest
assembled for your grand tour.

Liniment of Boyne shank,
the very digest of a salmon run,

a worm yawning in potato sap
and a maudlin whiff from tanneries

and distilleries on the Marsh Road.
But uncorked, languorous days still show

a girl with no straps to her dress dancing
in the sun and all that bustle filled

from some other source, so now you're
doubtful whether this really is Preston's.

TATE WATER

If you ask how a colour might come about,
consider the enigma of water determined by sky,
and by water I don't mean pool or rain barrel
but the wide expanse of sea or lake.
As with all things, this will depend
on where and when you look
because water absorbs light, and sea water
absorbs the larger truths of late evening
greater than the timid blue of morning.
So if sunlight entering the sea is filtered
until mainly blue and then washed back
to the observer above, who could be you
dawdling on cliff or private promontory,
then, like you, a stain of light depends on impurity
just as your purplish skin for cold or bruise
like a Doppler note brightens and passes and fades.
And if pine lakes deliver a bluish tinge,
remember in that water, increasing salts or acids
can make of the scattered light a trawl from pale
yellow to darkish brown, and, when peat is washed
down, sunlight may lose itself, cannot scatter,
and the lake becomes black. I can tell you,
impasto giving weight, how to make a profession
of mute things, but remain at a loss to figure
how the weight of water can be so sinister.

THOMPSON & THOMPSON

The stenographer's touch-typing
has me in thrall. The case

is the case in point
but her Remington is all.

She pouts, she doesn't drop
a stitch and I am aghast

to realise, so late in the day,
that the Thompson

who gave her the lowdown
on shorthand and what's written

on the body, was the Thompson
who tapped out bullet points

for his other Remington –
the Chicago typewriter.

THAT NOTE

Like Miles Davis' dark Arkansas roads
the tone I was after lay listless and dreaming
as we rode the sea lanes deep in Dublin Sound.
On either side of the waters we were crossing
lay cable, freight line, pipes of city joy,
and barely visible, though gleaming and new,
an audible pitch of beads and corded wire —
weird acoustics slumbering in their alloy.

And I knew it was there, like the shudder
in a mass light-years away shows
the hidden path of a polished ball of ice
come this way with its heart on fire.
And then that solder, that rich conspiracy of brass
and copper, a flame in the blood unlike
the one-art melancholy of a cedar grove
or the straight-on certainty of a 30s autobahn,
so it feels like time itself, or a bolt
from its legions, has come to this span we inhabit,
to count on and improvise, that note.

WHITE PAGE

Though the hospital nearby failed to register a temperature,
a moon rose and was full. Records show

ruffed up ranks of commonage and from asylum lots,
iris, lilac and ivy-covered trees. But these yellow fields,

with their memory of olive and cypress, tell nothing
of why he came, or why he placed an easel as dusk was setting,

nor can I gauge the hundreds of trivial impulses
coming together in their species of colour.

And through all the snows and all the winters, chalk lines list
so the very subject is lost in the accretion of tots and
    thimbles-full

of white spirit, just as the music stitched in the braid of a river
is enough to tip an idea of order back to the still white page.

THE VERANDAH

Though the verandah was covered
in a patina of end-of-season hues
its primary colours were more in the way
of notional tints—sand, blown gravel,
sea salt—and there is more to this
than you might think, the scorched memory
carries on the wind to this day, as I stand
in the middle of a narrow road.

What's left is a shrinking cabin,
like Winslow Homer's *The Dinner Horn*;
got up to sing perpetual summer
as now in league with bindweed and ivy
and a young woman calling 'time',
I begin to embrace the scattered look,
cap set to the promises of others,
and then that shift while attention
runs out on a serrated scroll
at the edge of someone else's life.

THE SILENT BROTHER

Here I am, come closer,
a diminutive figure

etched in straw,
nursing the trivial

comings and goings
that will never amount

to anything.
And if company bids welcome

and the spirit withdraws,
what shrinks away

is that riddle of diminishing light,
intrigue from backyards

and honeyed winter heat,
a fleece within fleece

for the sake of a circus of sparks.
But what I do know:

like a seed stitched
in a Dutch merchant's wallet

awaiting its bead of dye,
all music lies adjacent to music

and I can live for days
in the spell of a Kyrie Eleison.

My handkerchief is blood-
flecked, I throw my whistle

to the crowd,
I am down to one key.

VARIATION ON BLUE NOTE

If a gourd adrift on a water meadow
levels the draught in an ocean liner,
the babbling shelves of bottled spring,
the sodden taste of smalt and beryl
should feed canals on our sister planets
and somehow yield a love supreme.

But pipes leak gas, roofs leak rain,
my blindfold phrases are tired and sprung
and dribbling back to their various parts,
the many slips that sink a ship,
port-wine stain, mizzling tributaries of vein,
feed the drip on the lip of my saxophone.
You may ache for a theme. I do not.
I love the self-fulfilling water butt.

WAKING TOM

Just as in life, watching in his house,
we have agreed to disagree,
then he hums from the Irish,
'I am asleep, do not wake me'.

WEEKEND AWAY

Running a lexicon of cold and thaw
our hotel whinnies in its vatic store.

If you croon your stolen music,
I'll hum the cantata from a Japanese opera

and like shy samurai
we'll leave this world with a cosy virus

clutching a jar of wild honey
to nourish our sleep in the ocean.

But if we should drown in our own fluid
and our almanac of phrases

unravel the signature of influenza—
let that helix of clefs and quavers,

embalmer's script in Indian ink,
compose our spirited gavotte.

WHAT MAUREEN KNEW

Like the pitch of a Stradivarius, a lush tone cannot rely
for explanation alone on varnish or tanning,

and if I'm confusing how we come together with the vagaries
and chance of local weather, and if she appeared to prefer

the elegant sun of the bleached Alpine, in what locals call
'the forest of violins', then like something raised free range

she could emit such charcoal and honey, sufficient in voice
to remain, as her company dwindled to a few feeble outriders

weighted with ribbon and nickel. Her winters were long
and severe, her summers cold and wet, she fed

on teeming shellfish, ice-skated near Islandbridge,
lit braziers on the frozen Liffey mouth

and found in the sally banks a world that could resonate
in the off-beat of a high-hat. And whomsoever she took

in her arms, she would chase down the lines that loll
on the coasters of an ironic equation, and leave no trace.

But the day she clutched a sweepstake ticket in a legal office
in Nassau Street in 1931, offering the camera a smile as false

as her future, was the first to hit home like a residual flower—
we should not all make of our lives a scented bower.

WHO SPEAKS

Like the Mexican boy on his Appaloosa
when asked of the 'run-off',
or 'when it happens', silent in Spanish and English,
nods to affirm – mostly at night, at different
places, different amounts each time.

Or my leaving a building through plate glass
just before the company says
their logo may as well be parallel strips of Velcro
for all the effort to find the correct door
with my purse strings and amphetamines.

NEWFOUNDLAND TIME

Round the planting of the Gort oak
the true magnetic poles began a variation.
Ignoring the jolt of our millennium
they reclined briefly in the Pacific Ocean
down near the island of Guam.
But when they cradled the spine of Siberia
they passed all understanding, only to emerge later
in the belly of King William Sound.

On my aimless navigations of the midland
and western bypasses, sleek asphalt
like black streams amongst saplings,
I can gain the half-hour of daylight
like the half-hour I mislaid
when I once crossed from Nova Scotia
into the bosom of Newfoundland.
So when I recite the litany of true verticals
I can realign and slip through the fissure
that folds back, not at the open field
nor at the forest, but at the border between.

Slip Road

MISCHIEF AT THE GLOBE

A freckle spread on the scapula
of Cleopatra's lady-in-waiting

could be the ghost of Cassiopeia,
a flock of little pearls, a cuckoo spit,

or more likely, the intruder tattoo
of incipient melanoma.

And it's settling in for the long run
as well it might, since like us all

its host appears in the programme
as one of many players.

Through open doors for
entrances, exits and returns,

for legions racing in the night,
the Thames' traffic steals on—

barges going home to wharfs
and gardens, tugs heading down

river to safeguard their charges,
a starstruck muddy tide

sweeping the embankments,
all the night hollows

and all the weary singsong,
while here a girl in love with

mischief, seems more than willing
to vie with her mistress,

as every night she dares to sup
drains and dregs from a poison cup.

BALLYNAHINCH STATION

The caboose that came to rest in a siding of bog cotton,
will wait for ever to be back hitched to the whistle
and shunt of the Clifden train. Years now, since I stood
on Cashel Hill waving flags to Heart's Content,
and years since I worked a passage on the Great Eastern,

its great ballroom hollowed by gout, as it payed out
the working man's cable, to tell how clouds foam and toss,
and how small craft salt in brine for less.
Through a score of winters I harvest pulses and beets.
I get around in an old pick-up (rinsed Leitrim plates),

and when I've had enough of Beiderbecke and Waits,
I rest my ear on what's left of the rails, to riff on the tremolo
of grumbling rolling stock, the sobs from tinder stick pines
felled and felled again, while farther down the line
on a solitary angler's beat, minor chords play out

their lazy three/four time. And if bridges hereabouts
no longer hold sway, and if all of this is passing me by,
on the grassy platform of mustard seed and nettle,
I can still hear the signal, of an old girl in Euston,
with her one-way ticket to Ballynahinch Station.

A SHANNON BOATYARD

Close to the lake but not too close—
the Shannon could never rise this far—

a galvanised door that bangs and moans
and never quite regained its running order

now tacks and flaps like a ruined sail.
Deserted in a bright November afternoon

where rising up a late harvest moon
plays shy with the inebriated sun

dozing on a white horizon. Inside
a perished boneyard dreams of the alkaline

Sonora near Tucson and Abilene, and the deft
daft mothballed names of recompense

chilled by winter's wiles and frosts
recall a tungsten fog toughening the water

raising anti-fowling clear of the diesel smear,
bowline on a bight, cleat hitched,

timbers groaning, buckles straining at their stays
and that worrying buoyancy of anti-freeze,

letting go. Awkward on their stirrups and stilts,
cruisers kiss and hug, nose to arse and back again,

Marni, Lady B, little honest dreams
with still room for the ghostly seaplanes,

early mail carriers along the far flung,
all our slips for repair and all hiding out

from the false god of winter, to come again
in this fireside reading of the lakes.

THOSE DAYS

I used to stand on my porch
and see as far as three days' walk,
but those days are long out of reach.

Near-sighted now, a concave earth
seen through crushed sand
has a bevel line to show its worth.

It used to be that I could see far away
and that partly still holds true,
but shortened sight, reined in everyday

is what constitutes the matter now.
Soon everything will be at arm's length —
luger, shot, remote, fretted brow —

enough to make me want to stay,
more than enough to be going on,
but dreaming in the far away

chasing what remains in light,
passing over lost sunken fleets
I will be sent for, soon, at night.

THE BLIND COMMUTE

In this broad church of reeds and grasses,
at the north-west tip of Booterstown Marsh

two marker posts wait for a lick
of Hammerite or windy gloss

to cosy up like a ruined script,
to connive in a channel or spit

like that cut from Leitrim Village wharf
or the eel-like shimmy of the lonely

Scariff River, but stall mid-sentence
bumping up against the blacktop

of an endless grey-green Bayeux
scrolling tall tales from ribbons of chrome,

a tickertape stuttering morse
like mustard seeds snagged in a fingernail

or a path to nowhere trying to atone
with false exits blurred in mist and rain.

LESSONS IN NAVAJO

It could have been that rich brogue I overheard
on the fire escape of a walk-up, looking out on the halogen-lit
pock-marked asphalt, half-built back parking lot

of a midlands public house. And more hooch
than real contraband. But a stain lingers from the early
diamond white cold, where that late lost jarvey,

one over the eight, knelt to flush and flood pistons,
resorting at last to crank handles and those oaths you expect
from a man who knows too much, or just enough, of some

never written down Navajo. At some stage he wheeled
away in his buckled charabanc, as I, drifting from sleep,
salted half-remembered choicer cuts to practice in future

company, in that selfsame order of beer and bitters,
still and whiskey. Now it feels closer to the battlefield cipher
branching in the shipping lanes of the Pacific theatre,

where there was real purchase in a zigzag or stagger,
and the last of the Navajo nation, swept a safe path home
spouting babble and baffle and sweet talk.

AND I LET IT GO

This a story that needn't be told,
it has no consequence, no resolution,

and the few bored witnesses walking
the late afternoon strand, are oblivious

or pointing, unsure what might
be amiss, and thinking they were

immortal and are now of course
all dead. A boy, me in fact,

followed a beach ball into the quiet sea,
treading water, bobbing forever

out of reach, crossing into a vacant calm,
out of the mild, into a chill,

and then out of the late afternoon
and what could only be a seductive

whispering. And fast as it seemed
to be mine, I let it go, turned back

to the ribbed sand underfoot,
the strollers stopping with some

concern now, and then a woman,
with her dusted apron, come out

to stand on the grassy bank,
in a breeze blown, light blue,

cirrus, sand shifting, pet July day,
and offering what, I cannot say.

But her hand was clasped over
her trembling silent mouth.

A LOST BALL IN THE LONG GRASS

When I can't sleep, I address the ball
on the short fifth at Carrickmines.
The old course; in the shadow of Three Rock

and Tiknock, below the abandoned lead mine,
and nearby Foxrock Village slumbering
in its folds of fat. The wind dies away,

and breasting a hump of gorse, the pin flag
slackens, as it did when milk came in a churn
and everyone knew their place.

The sea in the distance smells of coconut,
and farther off, lie Welsh hills and failure,
as I slice into the dimples where Warwicks

and Spaldings are long since lost in the rough.
All this as I stumble in the wolf hour,
for a drink of water or something stronger,

padding through my galley kitchen, which looks
out over the sheer walls and exercise yard
of La Santé. Inmates guard their sandy lie,

their links and dunes, and like a lost ball
in the long grass, I fall in with an unequal gaze,
outliers drifting on a treeless, parched veldt,

where in the time that would have passed
no matter what, a colony of allusions
pay homage to our solitary pilgrimage.

TOM KILROY'S BIG COUNTRY

Chuck Connors played Buck Hannassey
'the local trash' in *The Big Country*.

He imagined the village teacher
held a spark for him, or at least

for his character, so when Burl Ives
thought he could then see a way

to resolve the intimacies of water,
he advised his son – the same Buck –

'treat her right, take a bath sometime.'
Misunderstandings of course

but no harm done, since characters
must be allowed space to be foolish,

that is, to take off on their own,
if only to whistle or hop a *sliotar*

off a white-washed wall,
or dream of rustling cattle

across a range of barbed wire
down to The Big Muddy.

So as a match is a battle or a pitch,
or more likely a stage,

let the flight of a ball
or a passing fancy

summon noisy characters
from the very depths

to audition as they enter
in search of their author.

ORSON WELLES ON THE GINZA LINE

Like a lone rider lost and unafraid
    through canyons of steel and glass
I ride the boxcars and the rails.

Sliding doors open onto mounds and tufts,
    tannoys soothe and murmur in Japanese
and should this be our stopping off,

let sleepers rouse to harmonics like these—
    gathering winds, ribbons of lace,
souterrains for lost calligraphies,

blue night descending, out of the race,
    slipstreams and zither strings
in the arms of a rush hour embrace.

AFTER A SHORT ILLNESS

Bare-chested, fresh out of pomade,
he lies with a beat-up paperback
propped for the benefit of shade.

Lothario of seltzer, tight with the riot squad,
he remembers the Margate Lido,
art deco on the Bray esplanade.

Dozing in a cloud of powder and snuff,
he dreams where red brick stores
and gives back heat like a risen loaf.

For a brief lunch hour he can waive
paycheck, bus pass, toothbrush
waiting in its cup, the grave.

ALBRECHT DÜRER: *GREAT PIECE OF TURF*

I could have stayed in the street,
etched a perpetual summer with an arc
of London planes, or reassembled
from footprints in a petrified lake
a matter-of-fact rhino,

double stitch flapped
like chain mail meccano,
with posture set to trample
and overlook all of this.
But the *all of this* is any corner

of any waste patch of ground,
with its sprung herbal shape-shifters,
phosphates spun in a quiet lassitude,
an aerosol barrage to risk
excommunication or a peeling

summons, so that creeping bent,
butcher grass, foxtail
and promiscuous sawbriar,
might compose a roof of turf
like a moist hoard in seed sump.

So cast aside the sorrow of weeding,
there will be time enough
to fork at random. Get down
chin on the ground and take note
of all the winters steeped in this.

ARD NA MARA

Crossroads with the sea close by,
a *Boy's Own* radio play

heard on a weeping signal,
a bawn, a soda fountain,

and my adolescent frame
as brittle as a zeppelin.

In the July of *Rain,*
by the white kerb of The Neptune,

in khaki, in tented marquee,
Durbridge's *Melissa* on TV,

and the echo of a midnight bell
muffled in the foggy groan

of a cargo ship failing to navigate
more than the river mouth,

its captain ploughing a sandbar
hurrying to his mistress's bed

in Baltray, or a biplane
running on empty

eyeing the expansive strand
pretending like Saint-Exupéry,

mail must get through,
or this parody of bucket swings,

Anglias, Zephyrs and riptides,
but not a farthing for what

is loved in, the lost world
of shouts and cries.

BERNADETTE GREEVY'S LAST SONG

Having always aspired to the notion of heaven
and tiring of the tribal yoke,
the pratfall of pronunciation,
the depths of the provincial,
she returns to offer succour
and give a taste of regal pleasure
in this, our hour of need.

Commanding, *de haut en bas,*
the gold and gleaming interregnum,
a ghostly mezzo echoing snow and ice
through halls and music houses,
and in Bach's *Kommt, ihr*
angefochtnen Sünder,
savours one last note, rounded
and deep from the pudenda.

BUSBY BERKELEY IN THE HOLM OAKS

Still dark days pining for light
when a Vespa drone of chainsaws —
pulley strapped on migrant shoulders,
bandoleers with pearl apostles —
go criss-cross waltzing through
our borrowed acre of Holm oaks.
With their hauling stirrup pads
they swing in the leafy rigging
as if dressing an opera backdrop.
And just as our time
should be, and is, indifferent
to the oakline, and like a set change
reading from stuttered prompts,
they lop more than their usual
stray saplings, till one whole
timber bowl comes down,
curtains part, and decades
of pent-up light begin to warm
our cool January wall.
And when time itself bears witness,
the bandoleers in silent single file
accept applause as their due
taking back the Zen carmine,
from parterre, pit and gallery,
deeper, deeper and dimmer
till that diminuendo of nothingness
is unable to fathom an encore.

CHAOS THEORY

Nothing may well come of nothing,
but on this balmy day in the borough
I set forth, paintbrush in hand.

With my sneakers and work gloves
I check out the scuffs on
rubbish bins, bollards, benches

and those hard recliners—not so citizens
can linger too long of course,
since the mantilla crowd or militia

might spring from less. But things need
touching up, unnoticed soft corrosions
and creeping indents, can do

with a lick of turps at least. I'm not
defacing, but I do notice gradual paint
peeling, on tree guards, fire hydrants,

lampposts even. And those confessional
grills for butts, the postboxes
where I can bring back the inlay

of Regina crests, as the mottled green,
chipped and spritzed by dogs,
hides some half-baked graffiti.

Rust paint works best, primary colours,
even now and then a black trim.
I don't worry about the shades.

Blue is blue as far as I'm concerned.
In the next street there's a water fountain
and a kiosk. I think I'll need primer.

FALSE FRUIT

I keep my eye on the love life
of these solemn winter crowns
and when light becomes various,
return to the garden to root and mulch
their tubers, like blousy beasts
of kale and reed. Raking or turning

the sulky pits, I nose them out like truffles
with their albino breath and stage fright,
and bending over to force the pace,
I cover their face with a mottled drape
or cosy strip of carpet or cardboard.
For this medicinal false fruit I'm all

out of breath, as the puck's shoot
muscles into a chill that sharpens
and liquorish stems, purplish swelled,
reach out to be harvested
by my host of migrant shepherds
in a pre-dawn candlelight.

FOR THE LOVE OF HOPS

Tiptoeing on our new fence, put up in a few hours
by two Wexford men who barely spoke a word,

he parries with feint and riposte for the nuts
and black suet ball which we comically offer

as our offhand gesture to unravel the food chain.
And make no mistake, his bustle curled and flexed

has as much to do with balance as applause.
Boxing clever, this southpaw of a thought too far

may sup from our cup, but should the fence
succumb to rot for lack of a spit of creosote,

or the flaking gazebo shift ground in a thaw,
or his very own sense of self, mitts at the ready,

lean to feral out of boredom, tired of being
offered saucers of leftovers, then as often

as he steadies to go back to his stand
of holm oaks, he returns for one more snifter,

the lure of hops perhaps greater, in the upturned
optic of the birdfeeder's dispenser.

GREENE'S BOOKSHOP AND P.O.

Licence, stamp, postal order,
my ninety-year-old neighbour
has come to pay her dues.

In the smoke and bustle
of Clare Street, she reads
brass names as fiction

for bailiff or discarded lover,
and as she tries to undress legalese –
searches in land registry

births, marriages and deeds –
she remembers that summer
in Saint-Lô, a mutineer

sans-papiers, making the most
of what little we need to know.
As the mid-afternoon sun

honours stations, on roof box,
valley and rail, an errant sirocco
trembles the lip of her dress,

and she careers again
in an Austin K2, through the heat
of Normandy's ash-choked lanes.

HER CLOSED ACCOUNT

Signatures are all about intention—
'doesn't everyone know my name'?
For a short span there were glimpses
where outside stalled on the gossip

of civil war and university days,
pre-marriage hops, doing the continental
in holiday snaps. But here in future time
where the rest must wait in line

who pleads the case for a closed account
when the *billets-doux* are pre-signed?
Should the hand veer off the page,
let Marshalsea rules apply

since now in another frame,
malfeasance and ruin
are the currency of her small dominion,
sinking like a flooded atoll.

HUSTON ON SARTRE

Dreaming of McIntosh and Messenger
I waited for him to catch his breath.
A jumped-up wisdom tooth
filled one whole day with panic
and with little else in mind, our rambling
embraced a dream of becoming.
He loved the hunt, call to hounds,
back street clinics in mid-western towns,
fires started, fires put out,
lifeboats ditching bodies in a drought,
how jackets of flesh for the bones
of a littoral script chase the shadow
of a fox going to ground, an echo for
the malcontents, plague year evacuees,
and my list from Adrian Messenger –
the essence and the primary cause

IN THE FOOTSTEPS OF RICHARD LONG

A pair of shoes, footprints in river mud,
what I thought I saw in Bertraghboy Bay

when a flood of seawater
filmed a meticulous script,

or once on the Little Pigeon River
(wherever that may be) flat stones

laid neat on a bed, or added stones,
and where the Arctic Circle

breasts the Bering Strait,
pale limbs of driftwood

arranged in a lunar diadem.
Abandoned landscapes follow his eye,

combines rusting on half-cut fields,
corrugated sheds, old seed calendars

flapping on stern evenings
as sun-scalped farm labourers

dawdle in the weary lullaby
of wind-chime and copperline.

Let this high-end hobo speak
for rock outcrops,

or inclines on pilgrim paths,
but like the schooner curvature

of a kneeling Bedouin—cushioned,
forever in the dust—he'll always seek

one more mark, though feet
seem not a part of mind or heart.

DOORS CLOSING

I've always loved the elevator,
the way it comes when you call.
And I disdain that cardiovascular fad

of taking the stairs. You can leave
those heartbeats for afternoon
tea dancing. I keep vintage bric-a-brac

outback, analogue floor dials,
half-moon and full-moon, even a photo
labelled 'Elevator to Hitler's

summer retreat'. Cranky sometimes
like a dumbwaiter, unravelling yarns
with a whiff of grease and talc,

there may be some interlock issues,
like that woman who died
after being pulled into the shaft.

But riding an elevator is safer
than walking in a straight line.
I might worry about our towers,

dark most of the time, but then
I remember, a Pinkerton guy with shotgun,
protecting a lobby in Manhattan,

in the great 1936 elevator strike.
Let's be clear, you control
the elevator, you control the city.

WORKSHY

When Don Givens made off with a treble clef
from the USSR's hammer and sickle,
I was skiving off with the backroom boys,
though in truth it could hardly have been me
in that real sense, since I'd yet to make out
in the cause of employment or recompense.
Phibsboro Tower gave off its usual blank stare —
the north face of ambition perhaps —
as our comrades, out to test the rub of Dalymount,
made a fuss on those sheets of asbestos,
otherwise the stands. And there were even a few
who managed to leave the buff files
of sob stories from deserted wives,
to abseil in, while I foolishly enquired,
below that famous roar as to what was going
down up there that could ever have held
so many beguiled while giving so little care
to the punishing nutmegs of Giles and Brady,
Brady and Giles. And as if this were Subbuteo
on immaculate baize, the seasoned few
who attend out of duty from outlying steppes,
still passed hush-hush notes for future show trials
in some disputed offside. Left with the odour
of Don Givens' flicks and feints, and a sombre
nicotine pall from the Soviet bench,
I was unable to parry that insistence, and moved
to embrace the allure of long afternoons,
dozing and shredding files, while ignoring all talk
of futures, derivatives, or contracts for difference.

NIXER

A young man works on the roof of my neighbour's house.
In a summer of purple skies he carries the weight
of the Cold War, or whatever the script is asking for.
Enigmatic to each fault, he has no need to do other

than scan drawings on the page, resting in the arms
of his underwritten character. He shoulders tiles
and rolling felt, happy to be anywhere, laying low,
knowing he is under the radar of so many drop-offs,

script re-writes and wide-angle shots. When light
starts to fade in the droll September winds, he'll fit
the last ridge tile and disappear into the interior
of his own making, to come again some bright spring

morning, babbling about the weight of the parallax,
the joy of falsetto, as, carpenter-style, he slots a pencil
cigarette behind his ear, and on a roof defying the tightrope
walker, leaves a bead of smoke, as silhouette or signature.

ORTOLAN IN BALLYNAHINCH

Mid July, a deluge, a marriage
and a hillside church. Ample time
to dress a brace of buntings,

kept in the dark, blinded like lovers,
gorged on millet, grapes and figs,
then drowned in balls of Armagnac

and baked for however long
it takes to blanch a heart.
And if beneath the photographer's

cape, you taste another life—
liqueur-soaked rambles in the thermals
of the Pyrenees, grapeshot

through Sahara and Camargue—
let it be a ghostly flutter
or something approaching order

that has a yellowhammer hausfrau
rising to mind the heavens
and dust the stars into a paper bag.

OUR LITTLE LIFE

Hours of light and lethargy
and in this windy café, Feste
lays out tables in a linen ceremony—

napkin, fork, ceramic plate,
and a raised canopy, for what is here
in the comical October heat,

the outdoor midday meal.
Stagehands fill walk-on parts
as our guests reveal

the play itself, holding fast
in a bower of lime and buddleia.
And should the afternoon be cast

for Feste in full flight,
urging us with a scarce glance
to embrace his new *Twelfth Night,*

set each scene like no other,
and look up from scattered books
to watch your father and mother

arm in arm on a midday stroll,
so that transience, or what you will,
lays out the marriage sojourn.

PILGARLIC

Our parish lengthsman, years retired, has taken to spending
these hot days in his garden shed. I hear a tap dancer's
   hammering,
discordant notes limbering up like old man Stockhausen,
so when he soft shoe shuffles downtown, he has more than
   base metal
to scan the gutters or clear the drains from a long winter
   slumber,
more than a baton to tap the morse on his fontanelle,
and if he tips his cap, he is making for that other home,
where hymn is an amalgam of flutter and whisper, where
   rhymes
fall in with their echo and his music scans the tension of
   sound.

RITA'S VERSION

Her bird bath water is the colour of tea,
bone china gleams on a bedroom wall,
there's tarp folded on the verandah,
and polished linoleum in the hall.

On a sideboard near the ink stand,
her ear trumpet is horsewhip clean,
and family pics groaning in frames
hide a jet black Singer sewing machine.

Where once she scattered life
from an apron pocket, her old order
is now sufficient unto day.
An ounce of prevention a border,

and a pound of cure. She feeds cats,
feral strays, the ones who need
quiet sun spots. And she'll save
their musk and piss to chalk weeds,

mind mice to spare worker bees,
so clover pollinates, cattle thrive
and an empire planes wood for fleets
to venture forth and colonise.

SLIP ROAD
i.m. Peter Fanning

In the way that some paths are hidden
this one was an afterthought,
a back hand slipped through and almost

overcome with by-pass and motorway.
But then why shouldn't it remain
a grace and favour right-of-way

so when you regain the known route
and all signposts announce the faraway,
here the coy and wild are their own kind

and in forgotten bramble beds
the poppy lies down with the eglantine?
And as for those stray cars past their sell-by,

or unmarked trucks taking confident short cuts
carrying contraband to a lay-by,
it's a line of least resistance

and only visible from a long distance
and only then when a quickening sun
pierces a rain shower, making clear a fold

or tear. As narratives run out of width,
only occasional spaces light up memory
like a firefly dance, unobserved, unrecorded

and like our shadows standing tall,
my brother tucks his sleeves, anxious to be off,
his ribbon of time slowing to a rumour.

SNOWMELT

Supper talk was of last year's snow,
thaw was late, the mountains white
and now as June was growing old
the run-off might come overnight.

If we never pass this way again,
stand and admire an antiquated kilter,
the accommodations wood makes
with itself, and then as shelter

and then our landlord's brisk 'goodbye' –
isolated, garrulous pioneer,
minding his cabin bought mail-order,
shipped and delivered here

as a lonely script, this equerry
speaks of an attendant life, sublime,
'I might be living out
someone else's design' –

and as our highway thunders,
less than a notional block,
and new bridges speed us over
the gorge to another flat-pack,

posted, no doubt, from a hangar lot
near the foot of the Cascades, we race
the snowmelt, like the racket
in a locomotive's distant embrace.

ROOKERY

There's been a clearing in the gardens—
lavish sycamores, some holly and beech,
cut down in the dead of night.

And from such absences, local rooks
eye up the far canopies, leafy and windy
like Gaudí. Strung through top tiers

chichi nests appear, one-bed apartments,
'old world style', far from that 'young
family thing', and at a few thousand a month

or whatever, in these parts, a steal.
I viewed them and thought 'I should move
here', sea views, no more long commutes

and OK, the shower stall
is jammed up against the kitchen sink,
but that's how they live in Paris,

and should visitors pose a problem—
my sister for instance coming to stay,
showering three times a day—

I can retreat to the sushi bar next door,
bone up on the folly of space
and watch a weary sun play tricks

with a blank wall. Rooks take
to all this in a gloaming, swirling, settling
and re-settling, as just the usual

quarrelsome racket, until they can
vacate, break for their winter cover
and the marionette theatre of dreams.

TALL BOYS

In Leeson Street
we find ourselves
in a Georgian chapel of ease,
an elite mass rock,

in an Irish lexicon,
in a credo unravelling,
in ambivalent government attire,
we stand, genuflect,

stand again and disperse,
miming handshakes
and the bluster of concern.
What stains our hands —

March as before
whipped in a narrow light —
as we peer into
Fitzwilliam's forbidden park,

are the old yarns snoozing
beneath the clipped grass
and all the dead tall boys
who made the winters fast.

VANLIFE

I wear plaid shirts to art classes and commute
to colleges to make up a whole day.
I do cardio and calisthenics, spot jog,

skip an imaginary rope, and for in-house tricks
count taken breaths on the beat
of the 'Walk', 'Don't Walk' down the street.

I love all those strategies for packing a case,
recipes for meals on the go. I drive through
the shore silos but the real money,

like a string of Halloween flares,
is on the High Line beyond the Beltway.
I keep aloe plants in my van cup holder.

I've heard that walk and talk coffee is over
and done. I plug my phone into the dashboard
charger as if it were a heart monitor.

Lately I've noticed scattered stacks
with their *Simon of the Desert* savants
mouthing off and waving. But that's just

a distraction or a fad, and I remain Chaplinesque
and airy sitting down at my local bar counter,
in a world of Martini sticks and coasters.

WHICH SIDE ARE YOU ON?

A faithless Sunday, a walk from mass,
two or three in gabardines emerging
from July's sun, everything to play for,
misdirected kisses, a warm embrace
and then some. Or perhaps it's the mark
apprentices flourish with their trowels,
off the cuff charcoal where bakers might
lay the sign of the cross, or fishmongers,
fumbling their catch, setting finger
and thumb in St. Peter's grip, so the lazy eye
of each artisan, heeding the rumpus of civil
war pistols, is obedient as a cobbler's last.

THE NIGHT TELEPHONIST
i.m. Peter Delaney

A yellow bedroom, an empty cane chair,
inflections, colour, tone,
and that first great rule, *steal the image*
until you've made it your own.

Work a passage through old Europe,
hitching still a noble craft,
wind up spent, on Hydra,
say hello to Leonard for a laugh.

Come back with tall tales and rumours,
choose your poison in plain view,
medicinal amber in stubby glasses,
rum and coffee, just for you.

Join the outré crowd who can't sit still,
make love on the run, work nights,
resurrect those unruly long-lost calls
on a switchboard plug-in, bang to rights.

Send postcards with mercury tags,
lines of coke for Paul Klee,
fuse-wire, Duchamp style, to addresses,
catch up with the ghost of Kandinsky.

Distrust, discard the given narrative,
your stylus always stuttered on repeat,
keep posting those anonymous missives
and see what might come back.

Too tired to attend your one exhibition,
preferring to break in a new 12-string,
sourced in a pre-Haussmann warren
where Pierre Bensusan used to sing.

More your taste his fugitive recitals
in an Aungier Street upstairs bar back room,
he too, trying to make himself heard
through the hazy fog of a lost afternoon.

When the last buses are long gone home,
engines idling on a frosty kerb line,
chauffeurs snooze with the morning edition,
and milk floats jump with adrenaline—

let this be your time; a fox on the road,
the suit brigade still wrapped in sheets,
head for home as the dawn crackles
in a light that shines like a field of wheat.

THOUGH THE HOUSE IS DARK

Let tides roam with promise or never come,
my east coast swimming days are nearly done.
I try to live a good life, stay away from kings,
heed the confetti of plastic scraps
on the continental shelf of things.
So what if I hear griffins roaring
through the night, or see blooms of jellyfish
in a gossamer, gasoline twilight?
I can still count radio pips from forgotten
cosmonauts, hear half-lost subs
maintaining almost silence, or gaze
as zeppelins drag—however faint the score—
moonlit serenades from Glenn's big band
in tux in silhouette on the marine floor.

AFTERWORD

I think what Gerard Fanning wanted was a quiet life. The thought pleased him. In 1975, when we were freelance teachers of English as a foreign language in Barcelona, he liked living in an apartment on the outskirts of the seaside town of Castelldefels. It was winter. And it satisfied him one day when he found new students in the town of Gavà, possibly the least fashionable resort along the coast. He spoke about it often: that was what he wanted, he said, to have a few students in a town like Gavà, the class not too early in the morning.

In his poems, Gerard Fanning weighed each word and each phrase with quiet, exquisite care. He had an instinct for what a sound, a rhythm, would do. It was something like having an ear for music. But he learned not to depend solely on his own innate tact and talent for phrasing. He would need to test every line. What he did must not stray from the initial image that he wanted to explore, but he sought to surprise himself, and that involved revision and revision, adding, erasing, day after day.

A few times, he showed me how he worked. He wrote in biro in an ordinary A-4 size notebook, the sort that students used to take notes in lectures. He would begin by setting down some phrases and then he would tentatively add some more. I have no memory of seeing anything crossed out. He moved, instead, to the next page and wrote the poem out that was forming again. And then he added lines, or half-lines, or even words, often to the side of the page. And then he would move on, writing the poem out once more.

Secret histories interested him, laybys, lanes, back gardens, half-hidden paths, suburbs. He liked the three-line stanza: it could remain suggestive, tactfully incomplete. It tended, like Gerard himself, to resist large statement.

With several poems on the go, he would return to one of them, perhaps one that he had left alone for a few weeks. He would see what could be done. This could take him ten minutes or an hour. He was open to any arrangement of words that might come, but watchful too. He did not believe that a poem was a gift. It came from moments when the mind was open to anything suitable that might occur and when the mind was also at its most suspicious of easy solutions. He was interested in the thing itself, and then alert to the idea that the thing itself faded and became distant not only with time but because of the sheer shakiness of memory, the famous unreliability of language.

In his poem 'Ludwig, Ruth & I', he riffed on language's role in creating the gap between what was experienced and what was known – 'language alone / might lasso the blond interior or confuse / the world we live in with the words we use.'

When I asked him once to take me through a particular poem line by line, I realized that each phrase he used had a very precise meaning for him. And the meaning mattered; indeed, it mattered so much that he sought to find a way of both anchoring it and suggesting its implications, finding a tone for it that eschewed banality and sought instead to match sound and significance. The finished poem needed to carry what we might call an energy relaxed enough to satisfy him.

It took a long time for some of these poems even to make their way into draft form. He was never in any hurry to finish a poem.

Between October 1973 in University College Dublin and Christmas 1975, when he left Barcelona to go back to Dublin and begin work in the Irish Civil Service, I sometimes saw Gerard every day. He wore his reticence lightly. It was only afterwards I realized how little he ever spoke about himself. (In 'With Siobhán', he writes of 'talking of other people / never ourselves'.) I knew he had been ill, but he hardly even alluded to it. Because his family lived within walking distance of the University College Dublin campus at Belfield, I could drop by his house in the evenings. We would eat beans on toast.

He would talk about what he was enjoying on television — I remember he liked *The Rockford Files* — and recent films — I remember he loved *Chinatown,* a scene from which is invoked in the first stanza of his poem 'Who Speaks'. He liked Tom Waits and Loudon Wainwright III. (He was delighted by the lines: 'Dead skunk in the middle of the road / Stinkin' to high heaven'.) Only once, when I asked him about the source of inspiration for a line, did he mention how much he admired Elgar's *Cello Concerto.* We never once spoke of Wittgenstein.

In the mid-1970s, he began to learn how the play the uilleann pipes, which are notoriously difficult. By the time he went to Spain, in October 1975, he had perfected a number of tunes. In the same way as he would disappear into his room to work on poems, he would go there to play the pipes.

He could seem diffident, but he had definite views on songs and films and paintings. And, of course, on poems. What we mainly spoke about were poems. One day in the early summer of 1975, I bumped into Gerard in Belfield, and he told me that he had secured an early copy of a new book of poems by Derek Mahon called *The Snow Party,* and, if I was free later, I could stop by his house and we could have our usual baked beans on toast and read the poems.

We already knew the last and longest poem, 'A Disused Shed in County Wexford', because it had appeared in print first in the magazine *Antaeus* and had developed the same status as Philip Larkin's 'Aubade'. Both were copied by hand to be given around. Mahon's poem had, by 1975, a kind of mythological status.

That evening, we devoured the book, going slowly through every poem. Gerard continued to admire Mahon, as he did Seamus Heaney and Paul Muldoon. But his reading in poetry was wide, and his influences were often surprising. I know if I met him and asked him if I was really hearing echoes of Wallace Stevens in lines from one of his poems that I most admire, 'Tate Water'—'water absorbs light, and sea water / absorbs the larger truths of late evening / greater than the timid blue of morning'– he would insist that the lines had come to him free in the air or they had their roots in some popular song or lines from a movie. But he could also have been absorbing Stevens. You could never be sure.

I can't remember a conversation about Borges, but Gerard would have read him as a matter of course. Borges's stories were part of the atmosphere of that time. In 'The Exactitude of Science', a one-paragraph story, Borges wrote:

> In this empire the art of cartography had reached such a perfection that a map of a single county covered a whole city, and a map of the empire that of a whole county. Finally, a point was reached when these colossal maps were no longer considered satisfactory, and the institutions of the cartographers made a map of the empire which was as large as the empire itself and coincided with it point for point.

I think Gerard loved the ironies in this passage, the sly humour. And then the idea of maps as living, sentient objects entered his spirit and made its way into his poems.

In 'Offering the Light', for example, 'the real map of Dublin / is about the same size as Dublin.' And in 'Philby in Ireland', he wrote: 'Somewhere in this parallel of workings / men catalogue the labyrinth of the city'.

Just as he was fascinated by maps and map-makers, he was intrigued by the lives of the great explorers. He liked to put a lone figure moving ominously or innocently in a strange place and see what might happen in a poem. His figures tended not to be poets but imposters or spies, men living the 'dual life', such as Kim Philby or John Stonehouse. Often, Gerard's landscapes came from memory and experience—such as the coast of north County Dublin or places in Canada he had visited—but often they were unnamed, haunted places. He was interested in codes and signals. He ended 'Occupations', a poem about the German bombing of Belfast, with:

> In the confused fires we build
> a tatter of signals:
> our life's definition now,
>
> a tired odyssey in a world
> grown warm with our cold grip.

In the time when I knew him best, Gerard seemed to have found a form that suited him. And it would have been hard then to have imagined him writing sonnets. He would have found the word 'sonnet' itself pompous. It surprised me then when sonnets began to appear—'The Quaker Wall', 'Trail', 'Homage to George Eliot in New Hampshire', 'Still Man', 'Frank', '22/09/07', and 'Though the House Is Dark'. Also, as Gerard worked on his first book, he would have been uneasy about using rhyme. Again, it suggested something alien to his sensibility; it suggested 'poetry', something made to impress. But, then, quietly, almost stealthily, Gerard let rhyme enter his poems, not as part of a pattern – he would have been unhappy with the notion of pattern – but as something organic, a sudden turn in the process of making a poem that seemed right.

He would not have embraced Auden's idea of poetry as 'memorable speech'; he sought a poem that was more shadow and less show. But, when he used rhyme, he created memorable speech without any obvious effort, as in lines like:

> but dreaming in the far away

> chasing what remains in light,
> passing over the sunken fleets
> I will be sent for, soon, at night.

Or in the last four lines of 'The Tan Spirals', with their opaque reference to cancer:

> Their song is like a faint cry,
> that first ache in the rogue cell,
> as though memory could ever justify
> all we had yet to tell.

When he sent me the poem 'Canower Sound', I was shocked by what a departure it was. His poems up to then had been coiled around their own form. It was not as if they were obscure or especially difficult, but their syntax and word-choice could often be textured and dense. I wondered if he had been listening to Erik Satie. Each section was just two lines, a thought, an image, playing between the conclusive and the inconsequential. In Gerard's earlier poems, I felt I knew where the power was coming from; in these poems,

I couldn't tell. It was partly the disguise of the throwaway, but it was also a sort of command over sound and whisper, an ability not to push the rhythm too hard, to leave well-enough alone, to produce a haunting after-effect without seeming to do so.

It made a difference that 'Canower Sound' was first published in a small edition. It was a poem to be passed around. Appearing now in this book, however, its power is more loudly manifest. While Gerard Fanning worked on his poems tentatively, like an explorer, he didn't finish them in that spirit. He would not let them go until he was sure about them. He learned to trust the breadth of his imagination and the scope of his own judgement. In doing so, he produced poems that are among the best written anywhere in the past half-century, poems like 'An Evening in Booterstown', 'Orienteering with Elizabeth', 'Preamble', 'Art Pepper Remembers Paul Desmond', 'Canower Sound', and 'Tate Water.'

   −Colm Tóibín

INTERVIEW WITH CONOR O'CALLAGHAN, 2013

By way of background, what is the earliest poem in this selection? Can you remember when and where it was written, and in what spirit? More particularly, what do you recall of Ireland and its poetry at the moment of composition, and of how you defined your creative ambitions starting out?

'Waiting on Lemass'. It was written in my parents' house in Dublin in the early 1970s. I had published some poems in undergraduate magazines and broadsheets (do they exist anymore?) and was trying to finish work to send to David Marcus' 'New Irish Writing' page in the *Irish Press*. As was his impeccable style, he replied immediately, and his encouragement was the spur I needed.

In those days there were independent bookshops (do they exist anymore?) – the Eblana, Parson's, Fred Hanna which stocked and stacked high publications from small poetry presses. The Dolmen Press accepted occasional first collections but was in decline, and though Thomas Kinsella had left for America, Austin Clarke could still be seen in the bookshops around Grafton Street. Seamus Heaney's and Derek Mahon's first books had appeared and further afield the major influences (do they exist anymore?) were Bishop, Gunn, Larkin, and Lowell.

Early 70s was definitely a different Ireland and many of your landscapes in Easter Snow *seem to pre-date 1992, the year of publication. 'Waiting on Lemass', for example, maps the exquisite tedium of a childhood in 1960s Ireland. If the earliest poem was early 1970s, and your first book appeared in 1992, it must have felt as if several collections were compressed into one?*

Exactly. And too much freight added, at times. 'Waiting on Lemass' deliberately confused Seán Lemass and Alex Leamas, the main character in Le Carré's *The Spy who Came in from the Cold*. The film version was made in Smithfield in Dublin. They needed a cheap location that resembled bombed-out Berlin. It was made in grainy black & white (what great colours they are) with Richard Burton and Claire Bloom—real exotica in Dublin at that time, Burton and Liz Taylor downing pints in local bars. The tedium you mention was real but only in a 50s and 60s childhood sense, where church and state had genuine control. By the mid to late 60s that seemed like so much froth and everything was possible.

By the late 70s, most of my contemporaries seemed to know exactly what to do about getting a book deal, but my output was always an issue. As soon as I gathered 25–30 poems together I would start deleting them in fives and sixes as not suitable, and so never seemed to reach the required figure to interest a publisher. In short, a lot was discarded, a lot compressed. It finally got to the stage in 1990–91 that friends were losing patience and encouraged me to send something to John Deane at Dedalus Press, and he agreed to publish *Easter Snow* in 1992. I'm not sure what ambition I had for the book, but it was very kindly received.

Speaking of Le Carré, several of the poems in Easter Snow *adopt the grammar and drama of superior spy novels and film noir; the man alone and nameless and working undercover. Le Carré, Graham Greene, John Buchan… Can you say something of what attracts you to this figure and how it adapts to poetry?*

More likely film noir. I like the confused look of 'the not too bright' private eye. Or just confusion, wrong man, wrong place—Greene's *Our Man in Havana*. In the TV version of

Tinker, Tailor, Soldier, Spy the civil service mentality was amusing, that dull quotidian stuff. Nearer the mark might be Mahon's 'The Last of the Fire Kings' – 'the man / Who drops at night / From a moving train / And strikes out over the fields / Where fireflies glow, / Not knowing a word of the language.' Making it up as you go along.

From what you're saying, you seem to get some kind of imaginative buzz out of that persona of nameless, faceless civil servant. Is this fair? Your second book is Working for the Government. *A lot of poets never write about their real jobs. There is a definite tradition of Irish poets who worked on behalf of the state: Denis Devlin, Dennis O'Driscoll… Are your colleagues aware of your other life? Or is poetry a version of secrecy, of being undercover, for you? In purely practical terms, how does the poetry fit into the life of a civil servant? And how does that work translate to poetry?*

The faceless civil servant might be a little too Kafkaesque but there is a permanent government or class who wield power and say nothing. Having a job gives me the prosaic cash to just get on with things. And so, for now, it's the 'in tray' as 'the lights come on at four, at the end of another year.' The 'Working for the Government' title was a nod to Talking Heads ('Don't Worry About The Government'). I have never worked 9–5. The job is outdoors, which involves visiting businesses, interviewing, and field work. It's a bit like a benign *Glengarry Glen Ross,* sharing anecdotes with colleagues; when I'm back, writing up in the office. This freedom has a maverick quality, with all the foolishness that entails. Eccentricities such as poetry are easily accommodated. If there is a covert, subversive quality to the other life of poetry, you do it in your head, on the bus, observing all the time. The job stuff is a progression from 'Toads' to 'Toads Revisited' and no harm in that.

Apart from those you mention, there were poets such as Valentin Iremonger and Richard Ryan (whom I met a few times) in the diplomatic corps. No doubt, they too grabbed the time for writing regardless of how the crust was earned.

The density of reference in some of the second book's poems might baffle some American readers. Can you describe the peripheral landscape of 'July in Bettystown', and say, perhaps, what the ever-present sea represents in your imagination? In 'The Fifties Parent' the image of your father is conflated with that of Nikita Khrushchev. Is there a Cold War sensibility in your work, where provincial life is loomed over by super powers, as in Muldoon's 'Cuba'? I suppose I hear it too in, again, the Fleming reference.

I've always lived beside the sea. Here in Dublin, and all childhood holidays twenty-five miles or so north of Dublin, where we rented my aunt's house each July in Bettystown. At that time, Bettystown was little more than a string of summer houses, a bump in the road, but it had a few shops and a hotel, and for me, a certain naive Rockwell quality. My older brothers were beginning to drift off to London etc. So the rest of us spent every day on the beach, swimming, making dams, smoking, the usual ten-year-old stuff. We seemed to be living as insignificant dots, while the real glamour was starting to relay back from my brothers settling in to London. Later at UCD I realized Ronan Sheehan and Neil Jordan were writing their first fictions about the same area.

The impressions laid down in those years, the colour and smell of the sea and the sky, barley fields stretching back from the dunes, horse racing on the strand, are like something from Alain-Fournier's *Le Grand Meaulnes*. All gone now, of course. This was the time of Kennedy's White House and Khrushchev's Bond villain. And my bald father hovering, smiling and seeming to say, 'everything will be all right'. If I was too young to understand the Cold War, it did pervade the times, even in sleepy Bettystown.

What is 'Murphy's Hexagon' that it should merit a revisit? The tidal nature of Omey seems to make the sea, in this poem at least, an ever-present symbol of inevitability and chance. Wasn't MacNeice's father partly reared on Omey? Also, can you say something about the form: the long lines and the couplets and the series of rhetorical questions?

I was with a group in the early 70s that included Patrick King. He was starting to publish poems and knew Richard Murphy. I had just got a car and we decided on a whim to drive over to the west of Ireland. Murphy had a slight mania for boats, Galway Hookers and the like, and building and doing up houses. He writes about it in his collection *The Price of Stone*. We heard he had built a small one-roomed house in the shape of a hexagon on Omey Island. So we drove across, looked in the window and there he was reading. He invited us in for a cup of tea and gave us each a neat signed edition of *High Island: Selected Poems*, from Harper & Row. You can only drive across twice a day, so I was keen not to miss the tide. The revisit was after King's early death, the house had been sold, and the more mundane domestic look of the place was the usual disappointment. There is a MacNeice connection on his father's side. As for the form, long lines seemed to suit the meandering journeys.

'Leaving Saint Helen's' and 'Quinsy'… Can you say something about the density of allusion in each of those two poems?

To misquote Larkin, 'illness is no different whined at than withstood'. I regard it as largely peripheral. Saint Helen's was a large Christian Brothers Novitiate at the end of our road. The young boys took their Sunday constitutional in groups of three. I heard later this was to prevent inappropriate relationships. It closed in the 70s and is now a luxury hotel. 'Quinsy' is more of a chancy thing, one thought borrowing another, ending with three 'X's'—kiss, illiterate signature, error.

'Working for the Government', the title poem of the second book, has something again of that faceless, nameless agent. But here the setting seems to be the West of Ireland, like so many of your poems. What's the gravitational pull there, both actually and in the poems? Also, money is invoked. I'm probably wrong, but much of the imagery at the heart of the poem seems to derive obliquely from the Seán Lemass soundbite about the rising tide that lifts all boats in relation to economics. I suppose, as with the other poets in the anthology, I am interested in those moments where the so-called Celtic Tiger is visible in the poem.

However naively, I thought Seán Lemass was modern and good for the country, though I know some people now take the view that the opening up in the 60s would have happened anyway. I started working in the 70s, a pre-computer age where all enquiries were sent by post, work entered in ledgers, carbon copies filed etc. etc. In my first year in the job I was transferred round the country at a day's notice, and for a suburban boy this orientation (disorientation?) was initially great fun, but ultimately became banal and tedious.

One of my first stints was to Clifden in County Galway. I was required to find and visit isolated farmers for various government schemes. The landscape just seemed to make sense, extraordinary light and colour with no shouting for attention. Tim Robinson, the author and cartographer based in Roundstone, captures it brilliantly. Also Eamon

Grennan in his poetry. The more you visit, of course, the more contacts and specific places resonate.

'Offering the Light', the first in Water & Power, *is a really beautiful little nugget. But, like many of your poems, it does need some unravelling. On the most basic level, can you explain the cricket terminology to a US audience and your attraction to it? It reminds me greatly of the gorgeous Douglas Dunn poem 'Close of Play', where cricketers leaving the field are likened to ghosts. Was this image evocative of a vanishing world for you as well? More specifically, what's the allure of dusk as a metaphor? Also, this wonderful idea at the end that the truest map of a place is the place itself; that a thing is its own best metaphor. Your rhyme 'Dublin' with 'Dublin'!*

I liked Roy Harper's early 70s hit, 'When an old Cricketer Leaves the Crease'–close of play, dusk gathering and a fleeting glimpse of a twelfth man at silly mid on. The poem uses a few cricketing terms. It's about a five-day test match, and play can be halted for a number of reasons. Rain, failing light, etc. Batsmen under pressure like the idea of abandoning play for the day. The quality of light can trigger the five lights on the pavilion wall to come on in sequence and when three are lit the umpires will 'offer the light to the batsmen'. The 'nightwatchman' is a safe pair of hands, put in to bat, near dusk, to guide the team safely through until the next day. Silly point is a field position close to the batsman and so, considered somewhat dangerous. There are, of course, some parallels with baseball. The final map image recalls a Borges short story. I liked the image of the dutiful/obsessive servant told to draw up a map of the city and as more and more details accumulate, the scale rises inexorably.

Can I ask you to explain the narrative of 'The Railway Guard'? What's happening in the poem? Can I ask you to say something, again, about the structure of the poem, how that impressionism

*of the passing landscape that the poem is flitting through is
created by image running into image, stanza into stanza? I
think there are only five sentences in a poem that's thirty-six
lines long. This and 'Stoney Road' feel close too in their attention
to inherited landscapes.*

It's one of those returning poems, years on and out of season.
Our transience, fleeting traces left in soil deposits and grasses.
In 1957 there was an explosion at the British nuclear power
plant in Windscale (renamed Sellafield), so there is a reference
to Geiger boys. News was more controlled then and we
heard nothing of any threat to milk supplies, food, swimming,
etc. There are the printed images of those summers fading
to white and a memory of a beloved, smiling, silent niece
joining my grandfather – who was the Station Master/Rail-
way Guard in Drogheda – and whom I remember visiting
when I was four or five. He rose to greet me from his fireside
chair, white hair, white whiskers, surrounded by a plume of
white pipe smoke. It's the only image I have of him. 'Stoney
Road' is a last image of my mother in old age praying for
release. She had had enough.

*'From Portstewart to Portrush' is real Derek Mahon territory,
not just geographically, but also in how it celebrates the 'debt to
pleasure in the mundane'. Our generation owes so much to
Mahon, doesn't it? In a way that might not be immediately obvious
to those outside of Ireland. Can I ask you to say something
about him, his work, its impact on yours, and what you think
he has added uniquely to Irish poetry?*

In 1998 there was a three-day conference on Derek Mahon
at the University of Ulster in Coleraine. My brother was
going up, and I joined him on a whim. It was a small gather-
ing, young academics on the make, like one of Mahon's own
strange sects in 'Nostalgias' – 'In a tiny stone church / On a

desolate headland / A lost tribe is singing "Abide With Me".'
Actually it was fun—though I found myself (like at school)
staring out the window at the routine rural doings and a
commuter train plying its trade, back and forth, between
neighbouring towns.

Mahon is now over 70 and yet there is remarkably little
written about him. Like Thomas Kinsella, he is *sui generis,*
the real thing. His tone is immaculate; he has a wickedly
sly sense of humor and is a wonderful reader of his own
work. He has led an admirable maverick existence outside
the comforts of the paycheck and pension, and if you stick
rigorously to the poems, he is an example to us all.

*Cinema is very important to you, isn't it? One poem references
Michael Cimino's ill-fated* Heaven's Gate. *The title poem
of your third book, though about your father's watch and its
demise while swimming, does also seem to draw on Roman
Polanski's* Chinatown! *Is this way wide of the mark? Isn't*
Water & Power *the LA civic authority that Jack Nicholson is
investigating? More generally, where do these references fit?*

Suburban cinemas were the norm in the 50s and 60s, and
my father used to bring me and my younger brother every
week to the local Stella until we could go on our own. In
1969 I went to University College Dublin in Earlsfort
Terrace and joined the film society. This was a crash course
in recent and classic European/World cinema—Truffaut,
Godard, Antonioni, Jancso, Forman, Malle, Bergman,
Kurosawa etc. It was a perfect grounding for the marvelous
new wave American films of the 70s and 80s. I liked
Heaven's Gate even if it was a little overwrought. Its intended
six-hour length might have done it justice. Like Welles' *The
Magnificent Ambersons,* the studio butchered it in a vain
attempt to recoup costs. And *Chinatown* is a marvelous film,

everyone on top of their game and a wonderful script. And you're right: the doomed Hollis Mulwray is the chief of the Water & Power Department. Corruption is a constant, but self-deception is somehow more interesting.

Can I ask you to say something about the form of 'Everything In Its Place', which seems to hover loosely between terza rima and villanelle? How does that connect, also, with what this poem (or any poem) is about? Those flush central rhymes kind of enact the rod mining for samples. More generally, what's your thinking of rhymes and stanzas? Do you decide before the poem begins, or does it happen naturally during composition?

For me, form nearly always asserts itself. There was a vogue a while ago for sestinas and villanelles. They all seemed very pleased with themselves in magazines etc., though somehow, the end result appeared worthy rather than the real thing. Mahon published an early villanelle, 'Antarctica', which is sensational. If you can't get that formal elegance and lightness of touch, it seems pointless. Sometimes in the attempt to complete a poem, rhymes and stanzas become insistent (or don't as the case may be). You can keep rewriting to avoid what might be a straitjacket, but form often persists and finally becomes a release. So 'Everything In Its Place' attempts a loose musical rhythm. A guy in a sky-scraper looks out at a building next door under construction, with a kind of inverted mining imagery. The rhyme simply fell into place.

Both 'The Cancer Bureau' and 'Quince', though the latter insists on non-belief, read as being as much about faith as anything more literal. Are poems acts, or paradigms, of faith for you?

Paradigms of faith may be a bit lofty for me, but perhaps if one eschews 'that vast, moth-eaten musical brocade' of faith, religion, you end up clinging to the wreckage of something else, then something else again. In 'The Cancer Bureau' I loved the idea of the load line and the plimsol mark, simple visual aids indicating cargo load. And the hospital nurse, casually drawing lines and tattoos on the body, diagnoses and balance. The poem ends with a faith in the world, as is. 'Quince' makes fun of the New Year resolution to get out more, plant more exotically and live off the consequences. If there is a sense of faith here, it's in weather and seasons.

Of the new poems included, both 'An Old Boyne Fish Barn' and 'Tate Water' seem to be about water and seeing. They dwell on the weight of things, whether it is 'the weight of water' or 'the weight of… vision'. I have asked the other poets this, so perhaps should ask you as well: what is the draw to light and water in your work?

I think we are a wee bit obsessed with both in these parts. The Boyne is a famous salmon run. What returns with each tide, however, is complicated by some 60-year-old leakage from Second World War munitions dumps in the Irish Sea. In 'Tate Water' the focus is more that water has no color in itself, but depends on various forms of light, though the putative narrator ties himself up in his own hubris and leaves the conclusion hanging. It could be more for a painter's eye, but that doesn't stop you trying to catch some of that rich transience. And it's where I live, the sea nearly always in view, the memory of foghorns, a cruel history of shipwreck and drowning and the harbour at Dún Laoghaire with its relics of empire and emigration. The changing light now seems less a feature of what we live in and more of a miracle, to be celebrated out of the everyday.

There are also two beautiful love poems: 'A Love Story' and 'In My Reading'. Both, though very different, seem to celebrate a wide-eyed innocence of seeing things as if for the first time. They also attempt to reconcile the world we do see and that glimpsed through borrowed sight, whether it be 'Mir's captain' or in books. Is there, do you think, a clearer celebratory note in your newer work? And can you say something about the difficulty of writing love poems?

Innocence seems correct, rather than a world-weary stale view. It's a tricky business though, and if it emerges as such, it seems more comfortable if it can exist of its own accord rather than carrying too much freight. Both these poems are simple enough, leaning a bit on whatever was to hand. If some poems take a few years to come into an acceptable focus and form, so be it. And if I'm celebrating anything, it's the joy of persistence.

Finally, can you say something about how you write a poem? Has it changed much over the years? Or is this something you prefer not to think about?

I do admire those who can plan the piece beforehand, set the parameters and style and with talent and discipline come up with the goods. My efforts are more like the child past bedtime, insisting on yet another glass of water. (We are back to 'water' again!) I think you once told me you like to get the correct last line. Maybe a bit too high-wire for me. But I think it's still true; you can get a line on a bus, a line staring out a window, a line of speech – something to get you going, and that could be some peace or a clattery café, and then there's music or rereading some poet who never disappoints. If I usually start with quite a long first draft I will often have to go back months later to find the original spark. So I still write in longhand. The pattern hasn't changed much and I wouldn't want to analyse it much either.

NOTES & ACKNOWLEDGEMENTS

Buíochas le Muintir Fanning agus le Muintir Uí Chuilinn, agus leis an gComhairle Ealaíon / *The Arts Council of Ireland* don tacaíocht agus maoiniú a thug siad to Gerard thar na blianta.

For their work and attention to this collection, thank you to Conor O'Callaghan, Gerald Dawe (i.m. 29/05/2024), and Colm Tóibín; all at Wake Forest: Alex Muller, Jefferson Holdridge, and interns Anna Gramling, Abby McCabe, Alex Silverio, Carson Smith, and Holly Thompson; Shannon Pallatta; Andy Fitzsimons, remembering Japan 2013; Gerry Smyth; Teresa Barrett; Dorothea Melvin; Louise Dobbin; Louise Ní Chuilinn; Jonathan Williams and Mary Peace.

Easter Snow

Poems first appeared in: Austin Clarke Broadsheet, *Cyphers, Connacht Tribune* (Writing in the West), *The Irish Times, The Irish Press* (New Irish Writing), *Krino, Paris Atlantic, Poetry Ireland Review, Rhinoceros, The Simon Anthology, Soundings 2, St Stephens,* UCD Broadsheet, RTÉ (The Poet's Choice, Appraisal).

Working for the Government

Poems first appeared in: *Dlí, The Honest Ulsterman, Krino, Poetry Ireland Review, Responding to Leopardi* (Dedalus Press), *Soho Square 6* (Bloomsbury), *Toward Harmony* (A Celebration: for Tony O'Malley: Dedalus), *The Whoseday Book.*

Water & Power

Poems first appeared in: *Agenda, The Irish Times, Irish*

University Review, London Review of Books, New Hibernia Review, New Writing 11 (Picador), *Poetry Ireland Review,* and in *The Rooney Prize—A Celebration* (ed. Terence Brown, 2001).

'Asylum Harbour', was commissioned by The Dún Laoghaire Harbour Board in 2003. 'Canower Sound', with drawings by Ann Bourke, was published in a limited edition by the Shinbone Press in 2003.

p. 129, 'Prayers at the Coal Quay': The *Leinster* sank off Dún Laoghaire, 10th October 1918.

p. 135, 'Like Stonehouse': John Stonehouse, the British Labour MP, who faked his suicide, 20th November 1974.

p. 139, 'Searching for Paul Henry's Sky': Meriwether Lewis and William Clark set off in May 1804 to explore the west of the United States. (Jonathan Raban, *Bad Land,* Picador, 1996).

Hombre: New and Selected Poems

Hombre included the following selections:

from *Easter Snow:* 'Waiting on Lemass', 'Travelling Light', 'Largo', 'Gas', 'A Diamond for Her Throat', 'An Evening in Booterstown', 'The Final Manoeuvre', 'Daytrip to Vancouver Island', 'Matt Kiernan', 'Film Noir', 'Philby in Ireland', 'Philby's Apostles on Merrion Strand', 'Sailing into Leitrim Village, 1986', 'The Lawn', 'The View from Errisbeg', 'Within a Mile of Dublin'.

from *Working for the Government:* 'Alma Again', 'Leaving Saint Helen's', 'Printing the Legend', 'Lenten Offering',

'About Abstraction', 'A Map of Crumlin', 'St. Stephen's Day', 'Art Pepper Remembers Paul Desmond', 'April 1963', 'Silence Visible on the Lough Inagh Road', 'Laytown Races 1959'.

from *Water & Power:* 'Offering the Light', 'A Carol for Clare', 'Ludwig, Ruth & I', 'Asylum Harbour', 'Teepee at Bow Lake', 'The Cancer Bureau', 'The Stone House: Dromod Harbour', 'The Railway Guard', *from* 'Canower Sound', 'Wide of the Mark', 'Everything in its Place', 'Water and Power'.

A number of edits were made to these poems, such as alternate line breaks, word changes, and adjustments to punctuation. This *Collected Poems* maintains the edits from *Hombre,* but places the poems within their respective original collections.

New poems from *Hombre* first appeared in: *A Meath Anthology, An Sionnach, Captivating Brightness* (Ballynahinch Castle Hotel/Occasional Press), *The Irish Times, London Review of Books, The Manchester Review, New Hibernia Review, Our Shared Japan, Ploughshares* (USA), *The Poetry Programme* (RTÉ), *Poetry International, Poetry Ireland Review, Southword, Sunday Miscellany* (RTÉ), *The Warwick Review* and *Wingspan: A Dedalus Sampler.*

'Prayers at the Coal Quay' and 'The Stone House: Dromod Harbour' were adapted by the composer Ian Wilson for his *Harbouring Suite* (2008).

p. 158, 'An Old Boyne Fish Barn': *You should have seen the sea in those days* (from Louis Malle's *Atlantic City*).

p. 171, 'Preston's': The last whiskey distillery in Drogheda.

p. 174, 'That Note': Written for the Sea Stallion Project.

Slip Road

'The Blind Commute' and 'Rookery' were first published in *The London Review of Books* (28 July 2016 and 4 January 2018, respectively).

'After a Short Illness', 'Busby Berkeley in the Holm Oaks', 'Chaos Theory', 'Workshy', and 'The Night Telephonist' were published in *The Manchester Review* (December 2017).

'Lessons in Navajo' and 'For the Love of Hops' were first published in *Poetry Ireland Review* (issues 119 and 122, respectively).

'Though the House is Dark' was first published in *The Irish Times* (13 October 2018).

Interview with Conor O'Callaghan, 2013

This interview originally appeared in *The Wake Forest Series of Irish Poetry Volume III*, edited by Conor O'Callaghan, along with a selection of 24 poems by Gerard Fanning:

from *Easter Snow:* 'Waiting on Lemass', 'Making Deals', 'Philby in Ireland', 'The Final Manoeuvre', 'Chemotherapy', 'Matt Kiernan', 'Travelling Light'.

from *Working for the Government:* 'July in Bettystown', 'The Fifties Parent', 'Murphy's Hexagon Revisited', 'Leaving Saint Helen's', 'Quinsy', 'She Scratches His Wrist', 'Working for the Government'.

from *Water & Power:* 'Offering the Light', 'The Railway Guard', 'Stoney Road', 'The Cancer Bureau', 'Quince', 'Water and Power'.

New Poems: 'A Love Story', 'In My Reading', 'Tate Water', 'An Old Boyne Fish Barn.'